Spanish Phrasebook for Business, Finance, and Everyday Communication

Jarvis Lebredo Lebredo

Houghton Mifflin Company
Boston   New York

Director, Modern Language Programs:
    E. Kristina Baer
Development Manager: Beth Kramer
Associate Development Editor:
    Rafael Burgos-Mirabal
Editorial Assistant: Nasya Laymon
Manufacturing Manager: Florence Cadran
Associate Marketing Manager:
    Tina Crowley-Desprez

Printed in the U.S.A.

ISBN: 0-395-96307-9

123456789-EB-03 02 01 00 99

Preface

Four pocket phrasebooks now accompany the successful *Basic Spanish Grammar (BSG)* communication and career manual series. Each provides handy reference word lists to assist students of Spanish for specific career purposes and professionals who use Spanish in the workplace, reinforcing the practical approach that this program has offered to Spanish learners for the past twenty years.

The *BSG* series includes a core grammar textbook, two communication manuals (the introductory *Getting Along in Spanish* and the higher-level *Spanish for Communication*) and five career manuals: *Spanish for Business and Finance, Spanish for Medical Personnel, Spanish for Law Enforcement, Spanish for Social Services,* and *Spanish for Teachers*. When used in combination with the *BSG* grammar textbook, the career manuals teach students the basic structures of Spanish and the vocabulary pertaining to specific professions.

As their titles indicate, the phrasebooks include the terms and phrases that appear in six manuals:

> *Phrasebook for Getting Along in Spanish*
> *Spanish Phrasebook for Business, Finance, and Everyday Communication*

Spanish Phrasebook for Medical and Social Services Professionals
Spanish Phrasebook for Law Enforcement and Social Services Professionals

Since many learners of Spanish for specific careers are English speakers, the phrasebooks include Spanish–English and English–Spanish listings. Designed for use in the office or in the field, these phrasebooks will provide a convenient resource for professionals who need a brief, portable guide to common Spanish words and phrases.

Abbreviations Used in This Book

The following abbreviations are used in the phrasebook.

adj.	adjective
adv.	adverb
coll.	colloquial
f.	feminine noun
fam.	familiar
form.	formal
inf.	infinitive
m.	masculine noun
Méx.	México
pl.	plural
prep.	preposition
pron.	pronoun
sing.	singular

Spanish–English

A

a to; at

  ¿— cómo está el cambio? What's the rate of exchange?

  — la derecha (izquierda) to the right (left)

  — la hora del almuerzo at lunch time

  — la llegada upon arrival

  — la semana weekly

  — la vuelta de la esquina around the corner

  — las (+ *time*) at (+ *time*)

  — lo mejor maybe, perhaps

  — medio día part-time

  — menos que unless

  — nombre mío in my name

  — partes iguales in equal parts

  — partir de starting, as of

  — partir del día as of (+ *date*)

  — pesar de (que) in spite of (the fact that)

  — pie on foot

  — plazo fijo fixed rate; fixed term (deposit)

  — plazos in installments

  ¿— qué hora? At what time?

  ¿— qué distancia? how far?

  — su cargo at your expense

  — sus órdenes at your service

  — tiempo on time

  — tiempo completo full-time

  — toda plana full-page

  — todo el mundo the world over

  — (tres) cuadras de (three) blocks from

— **veces** sometimes

— **ver** let's see

abierto(a) open

abintestato (*m.*) intestate case

abogado(a) lawyer (*m., f.*)

— **acusador(a)** (*m., f.*) prosecutor

abrazo (*m.*) hug, embrace

abrecartas (*m. sing.*) letter opener

abrigo (*m.*) coat

abril April

abrir to open

— **un negocio** to set up a business

abrocharse el cinturón to fasten your seat belts

absurdo(a) absurd

abuelo(a) (*m., f.*) grandfather, grandmother

aburrirse to get bored

acabado (*m.*) finished effect or appearance of a product

acabar to finish

— **de (+ *inf.*)** to have just (done something)

acampar to camp

acceso (*m.*) access

accesorio (*m.*) accessory

accidente (*m.*) accident

acción (*f.*) stock, share of stock

aceite (*m.*) oil

aceituna (*f.*) olive

acelerador (*m.*) accelerator

aceptar to accept

acera (*f.*) sidewalk

acerca de about

aconsejar to advise

acordarse (o:ue) to remember

acostar(se) (o:ue)   to put (go) to bed
acostumbrarse (a)   to get used to
acreditado(a)   well-established
acreditar   to accredit; to give official authorization; to credit
acreedor(a) (*m., f.*)   creditor
activo (*m.*)   assets
actual   current, present
actualmente   presently
acumulador (*m.*)   battery
acusado(a) (*m., f.*)   defendant (*in a criminal case*)
acuse de recibo (*m.*)   return receipt
adaptar   to adapt
adelantar   to pay in advance
adelgazar   to lose weight
además (de)   besides
adentro   inside
adicional   additional
adiós   good-bye
adjetivo (*m.*)   adjective
adjudicado(a)   awarded
adjunto (*m.*)   enclosure; (*adj.*) attached
administración (*f.*)   administration
   — **de empresas (negocios)** (*f.*)   business administration
   — **de Pequeños Negocios** (*f.*)   Small Business Administration
   — **Federal de Hipotecas** (*f.*)   Federal Housing Authority (FHA)
administrador(a) (*m., f.*)   administrator, manager
administrar   to manage
admitir   to admit
¿adónde?   where (to)?

aduana (*f.*)   customs
aéreo(a)   air
aerolínea (*f.*)   airline
aeropuerto (*m.*)   airport
afectar   to affect
afeitar(se)   to shave
afortunadamente   fortunately, luckily
afuera   out, outside
agarrar   to take
agencia (*f.*)   agency
    — de viajes (*f.*)   travel agency
    — de publicidad (*f.*)   advertising agency
agente (*m., f.*)   agent
    — viajero(a) (*m., f.*)   traveling salesperson
agosto   August
agrado (*m.*)   pleasure
agregar   to add
agua (*f.* but **el agua**)   water
    — caliente (fría) (*f.*)   hot (cold) water
    — mineral (*f.*)   mineral water
aguacate (*m.*)   avocado
aguacero (*m.*)   rainshower
aguafiestas (*m., f.*)   party pooper
ahora   now
    — mismo   right now
ahorita   now; in a while (*Méx.*)
ahorrar   to save (money)
aire (*m.*)   air
    — acondicionado (*m.*)   air conditioning
ají (*m.*)   chile (bell pepper)
ajo (*m.*)   garlic
ajuste (*m.*)   adjustment; reconciliation
al (**a + el**)   to the
    — año   yearly

— **detal** retail
— **detalle** retail
— **día** daily
— **día siguiente** the next day
— **final** at the end
— **fondo** in the back
— **gusto** any style, to order, to taste
— **horno** baked
— **lado de** next to
— **llegar** upon arrival
— **mayoreo** wholesale
— **mes** monthly
— **poco rato** a while later
— **por mayor** wholesale
— **por menor** retail
— **por menudo** retail
— **rato** later, a while later
— **respecto** about that; about the matter
— **ritmo de** acoording to
— **vapor** steamed
albacea (*m., f.*) executor
alberca (*f.*) swimming pool (*Méx.*)
albóndiga (*f.*) meatball
alcanzar to reach; to be enough
alcohol (*m.*) alcohol
alcohólico(a) alcoholic
alegrarse (de) to be glad
alérgico(a) allergic
alfarería (*f.*) pottery (*i.e., the craft*); pottery shop
alfombra (*f.*) carpet
algo something
   ¿— **más?** Anything else?
   ¿— **que declarar?** Anything to declare?
algodón (*m.*) cotton

alguien someone, somebody
algún(o)(a) some, any
  alguna vez ever
  algunas veces sometimes
alimentar to feed
alimentos frescos (*m. pl.*) fresh foods
allá there; over there
allí there
almacén (*m.*) warehouse
almeja (*f.*) clam
almohada (*f.*) pillow
almorzar (o:ue) to have lunch
almuerzo (*m.*) lunch
alquilado(a) rented
alquilar to rent, to lease
alquiler (*m.*) rent
alrededor de about
altavoz (*m.*) loudspeaker
alto (*m.*) height; depth (*of a container*)
alto(a) high; tall
altoparlante (*m.*) loudspeaker
altura (*f.*) altitude, height
amable kind
amarillo(a) yellow
ambos(as) both
ambulancia (*f.*) ambulance
amenazar to threaten
americano(a) American
amigo(a) (*m., f.*) friend
amor (*m.*) love
amortiguador (*m.*) shock absorber
amueblado(a) furnished
análisis (*m.*) test
ancho (*m.*) width

andén (*m.*)   (railway) platform
anestesia (*f.*)   anesthesia
anexo (*m.*)   enclosure
angosto(a)   narrow
anillo (*m.*)   ring
animal (*m.*)   animal
— **vivo** (*m.*)   live animal
animalito (*m.*)   pet
aniversario (*m.*)   anniversary
anoche   last night
anotar   to write down, to note, to jot down
anteayer   the day before yesterday
antefirma (*f.*)   sender's company name
anteojos (*m. pl.*)   eyeglasses
— **de sol** (*m. pl.*)   sunglasses
anterior   previous, former
antes (de)   before
— **de decidir**   before deciding
antibiótico (*m.*)   antibiotic
anticipo (*m.*)   advance payment
anual (*adj.*)   yearly
anunciar   to announce
anuncio (*m.*)   ad
año (*m.*)   year
apagar   to turn off; to put out (*a fire*); to stop (*a motor*)
— **la luz**   to turn off the light
aparcar   to park
aparecer   to appear
apariencia (*f.*)   appearance
apartado postal (*m.*)   post office box
apartamento (*m.*)   apartment
aparte   separately; in addition to

apellido (*m.*)   last name, surname
   — **materno** (*m.*)   mother's last name
   — **paterno** (*m.*)   father's last name
apenas   scarcely, hardly
apio (*m.*)   celery
aprender   to learn
apretar (e:ie)   to squeeze; to be too tight
aprobación (*f.*)   approval
aprobar (o:ue)   to approve
aprovechar   to take advantage
apurarse   to hurry up
aquél (*m.*)   that one (over there)
aquí   here
   — **tiene...**   here's . . .
árabe   Arab, Arabic
aranceles (*m. pl.*)   (customs) duty
árbol (*m.*)   tree
   — **frutal** (*m.*)   fruit tree
archivar   to file
archivador (*m.*)   file; filing cabinet (*España*)
área (*f.* but **el área**)   area
arete (*m.*)   earring
argentino(a)   Argentinian
arrancar   to start (a motor)
arreglar   to fix
arreglo (*m.*)   arrangement
arrendamiento (*m.*)   lease
arrendar   to rent, to lease
arrendatario(a) (*m., f.*)   lessee
arriba   upstairs
arrimar el carro   to pull over a car
arroz (*m.*)   rice
   — **con leche** (*m.*)   rice pudding
   — **con pollo** (*m.*)   chicken and rice

arte (*f.* but **el arte**)   art
artesanía (*f.*)   art craft; handicraft
artículo (*m.*)   article; item
arvejas (*f. pl.*)   peas
asado(a)   grilled, broiled, roasted
asalto (*m.*)   assault; round (boxing)
ascensor (*m.*)   elevator
asegurado(a)   insured; (*m., f.*) policyholder
asegurador(a)   insurer (*m., f.*); insurance
   company
asegurar   to ensure; to insure
asesinato del primer (segundo) grado (*m.*)
   first (second) degree murder
asesor(a) de inversiones (*m., f.*) investment
   officer
asesoramiento (*m.*)   advice; consulting
así   this way, like this, like that
   — que   so
asiduidad (*f.*)   frequency (*of business orders*)
asiento (*m.*)   seat; entry
   — de diario   journal entry
   — de pasillo (*m.*)   aisle seat
   — de ventanilla   window seat
asignatura (*f.*)   subject (*in school*)
asistencia (*f.*)   attendance
asistente (*m., f.*)   assistant
asistir   to attend
asociación (*f.*)   association
aspiradora (*f.*)   vacuum cleaner
aspirante (*m., f.*)   applicant
aspirina (*f.*)   aspirin
asumir   to assume
asunto (*m.*)   reference line; subject

atención (*f.*)   attention
— **médica y hospitalaria** (*f.*)   medical and hospital care
atender (e:ie)   to assist; to attend to; to wait on
atentado (*m.*)   attempt
aterrizaje (*m.*)   landing
aterrizar   to land (*a plane*)
atlético(a)   athletic
atropellar   to run over
atún (*m.*)   tuna fish
aumentar   to increase
— **de peso**   to gain weight
aumento (*m.*)   increase; raise
aunque   although; even though
ausencia (*f.*)   absence
auto (*m.*)   car
autobús (*m.*)   bus
automáticamente   automatically
automático(a)   automatic
automatizar   to automate
autopista (*f.*)   expressway; freeway
autorizar   to authorize
auxiliar de vuelo (*m., f.*)   flight attendant
¡Auxilio!   Help!
aval (*m.*)   collateral
avenida (*f.*)   avenue
avería (*f.*)   damage (*merchandise during transport*)
averiguar   to find out
avión (*m.*)   plane
avisar   to inform; to give notice
aviso (*m.*)   ad
¡Ay!   Ouch!
ayer   yesterday

ayuda (*f.*)   help; assistance
ayudante (*m.*, *f.*)   assistant
ayudar   to help
azafata (*f.*)   female flight attendant, stewardess

B

bacalao (*m.*)   cod
bailar   to dance
baile (*m.*)   dance
bajar   to go down, to descend
  — **se**   to get off
bajo(a)   short (*height*), low
balance (*m.*)   balance
  — **de comprobación** (*m.*)   trial balance
  — **general** (*m.*)   balance sheet
balanceado(a)   balanced
balanza (*f.*)   scales
balboa (*m.*)   currency of Panama
baldosa (*f.*)   tile
bancario(a)   (*adj.*) bank
banco (*m.*)   bank
banda elástica (*f.*)   rubber band
bandeja (*f.*)   tray
banquero(a) (*m.*, *f.*)   banker
banqueta (*f.*)   sidewalk (*Méx.*)
bañadera (*f.*)   bathtub
bañar(se)   to bathe
baño (*m.*)   bathroom; toilet
barato(a)   inexpensive, cheap
barba (*f.*)   beard
barbería (*f.*)   barber shop
barbero(a)   barber
barco (*m.*)   ship; boat

barrer   to sweep
barrio (*m.*)   neighborhood
base de datos (*f.*)   data base
básquetbol (*m.*)   basketball
bastante   quite, enough
basura (*f.*)   trash
bata (*f.*)   gown, robe
batería (*f.*)   battery
baúl (*m.*)   trunk
bazar (*m.*)   bazaar; store
beber   to drink
bebida (*f.*)   drink
beca (*f.*)   scholarship
beneficiario(a) (*m., f.*)   beneficiary; person or
   business authorized to receive payment (*bill of
   exchange*)
beneficio adicional (*m.*)   fringe benefit
berro (*m.*)   watercress
biblioteca (*f.*)   library
bicicleta (*f.*)   bicycle
bien   good; well; fine; (*m.*) good
   — **cocido(a)**   well done
   — **cocinado(a)**   well done
bienes (*m. pl.*)   assets
   — **inmuebles** (*m. pl.*)   real estate
   — **muebles** (*m. pl.*)   personal property
   — **raíces** (*m. pl.*)   real estate
bienvenido(a)   welcome
bife (*m.*)   steak
biftec (*m.*)   steak
bigote (*m.*)   moustache
bilingüe   bilingual
billete (*m.*)   ticket; bill, (monetary) note
   — **de ida** (*m.*)   one-way ticket

— **de ida y vuelta** (*m.*)   round-trip ticket

— **falso** (*m.*)   counterfeit bill

billetera (*f.*)   wallet

bisté (*m.*)   steak

bistec (*m.*)   steak

blanco(a)   white

blanquillo (*m.*)   egg (*Méx.*)

blusa (*f.*)   blouse

boca (*f.*)   mouth

bocina (*f.*)   horn, klaxon

boda (*f.*)   wedding

boleto (*m.*)   ticket

bolígrafo (*m.*)   ballpoint pen

bolívar (*m.*)   currency of Venezuela

boliviano (*m.*)   currency of Bolivia

bolsa (*f.*)   bag, purse

— **de dormir** (*f.*)   sleeping bag

— **de hielo** (*f.*)   ice pack

bolso de mano (*m.*)   (hand)bag, carry-on bag
(luggage)

bomba de agua (*f.*)   water pump

bombero (*m.*)   fireman

bombones (*m. pl.*)   candy, bonbons

bonito(a)   pretty, beautiful

bono (*m.*)   bond

borracho(a)   drunk

bota (*f.*)   boot

botar   to throw away, to get rid of

botella (*f.*)   bottle

botones (*m.*)   bellhop, bellboy

boulevard (*m.*)   boulevard

brazo (*m.*)   arm

brécol (*m.*)   broccoli

breve   brief

brillante (*m.*)   diamond
brindis (*m.*)   toast
bróculi (*m.*)   broccoli
broma (*f.*)   joke
bronceador (*m.*)   suntan lotion
bruto(a)   gross
budín (*m.*)   pudding
buen(o)(a)   good
  ¡Buen provecho!   Good appetite!, Bon
    appetit!
  ¡Buen viaje!   (Have a) nice trip!
  buenas noches   good evening, good night
  buenas tardes   good afternoon
  buenos días   good morning, good day
bueno (*adv.*)   well, okay, sure
bufete (*m.*)   office
bujía (*f.*)   spark plug
bulto (*m.*)   package, bundle
buque (*m.*)   ship; boat
buró (*m.*)   desk
buscar   to look for
butaca (*f.*)   armchair
buzón (*m.*)   mail box

C

caballero (*m.*)   gentleman
caballo (*m.*)   horse
caber   to fit
cabeza (*f.*)   head
  — de familia (*m., f.*)   head of household (of
    the family)
cacahuate (*m.*)   peanut (*Méx.*)
cada   each, every

cadena (*f.*)   chain
cadera (*f.*)   hip
caerse   to fall down
café (*m.*)   coffee; (*adj.*) brown
— **con leche** (*m.*)   café au lait
— **expreso** (*m.*)   espresso, strong black coffee
— **solo** (*m.*)   espresso, strong black coffee
cafetería (*f.*)   cafeteria
caja (*f.*)   box; cash register, petty cash
— **de bolas** (*f.*)   ball bearings
— **registradora** (*f.*)   cash register
cajero(a) (*m., f.*)   teller
cajero automático (*m.*)   automatic teller machine
cajetilla (*f.*)   pack, package
cajuela (*f.*)   trunk (*Méx.*)
calamar (*m.*)   squid
calcetines (*m. pl.*)   socks
calculador(a) (*m., f.*)   calculator
— **de bolsillo** (*m., f.*)   pocket calculator
calderilla (*f.*)   small change
caldo (*m.*)   broth
calefacción (*f.*)   heating
calidad (*f.*)   quality
caliente   hot
calificación (*f.*)   qualification
calificar   to qualify
calle (*f.*)   street
calmante (*m.*)   pain killer
calmar(se)   to calm (down)
caloría (*f.*)   calorie
calzar   to wear a certain shoe size
calzoncillo (*m.*)   men's shorts (underwear)

cama (*f.*)   bed
  — **chica** (*f.*)   twin bed
  — **doble** (*f.*)   double bed
  — **individual** (*f.*)   twin bed
  — **matrimonial** (*f.*)   double bed
  — **personal** (*f.*)   twin bed
cámara (*f.*)   camera
  — **de vídeo** (*f.*)   video camera
  — **fotográfica** (*f.*)   (photographic) camera
camarero(a) (*m., f.*)   waiter, waitress
camarón (*m.*)   shrimp
cambiar   to change, to exchange
  — **de idea**   to change one's mind
  — **un cheque**   to cash a check
cambio (*m.*)   change; exchange
  — **de aceite** (*m.*)   oil change
  — **mecánico** (*m.*)   standard shift (*automobile*)
caminando   on foot
caminar   to walk
camión (*m.*)   truck; bus (*Méx.*)
camioneta (*f.*)   van; station wagon
camisa (*f.*)   shirt
camiseta (*f.*)   T-shirt
camisón (*m.*)   nightgown
campaña de promoción (*f.*)   promotion
  campaign
campeón(ona) (*m., f.*)   champion
cancelado(a)   canceled
cancelar   to cancel
candidato(a) (*m., f.*)   candidate; applicant
cangrejo (*m.*)   crab
cansado(a)   tired
cantidad (*f.*)   quantity
caña de pescar (*f.*)   fishing pole

capacidad (*f.*)   means
capital (*m.*)   capital (*money*)
capó (*m.*)   hood
cara (*f.*)   face
característica (*f.*)   feature
¡Caramba!   Gosh!
carbohidrato (*m.*)   carbohydrate
carburador (*m.*)   carburetor
carga (*f.*)   shipment, load; title
cargamento (*m.*)   shipment, load
cargar   to charge; to load
cargo (*m.*)   title
caridad (*f.*)   charity
cariño (*m.*)   love (*term of endearment*)
cariñosamente   with love, affectionately
carne (*f.*)   meat
 — **asada** (*f.*)   steak (*Méx.*)
 — **de res** (*f.*)   beef
 — **molida** (*f.*)   ground meat
 — **picada** (*f.*)   ground meat
carnicería (*f.*)   meat market, butcher shop
caro(a)   expensive
carrera (*f.*)   studies, schooling; career
 — **de automóviles** (*f.*)   auto race
carretera (*f.*)   highway
carro (*m.*)   car
carrocería (*f.*)   body (*of a car*)
carta (*f.*)   letter
 — **certificada** (*f.*)   registered (certified) letter
 — **circular** (*f.*)   circular
 — **de negocios** (*f.*)   business letter
 — **de recomendación** (*f.*)   letter of
   recommendation
cartel (*m.*)   poster

cartera (*f.*)   handbag, purse; wallet
cartero(a) (*m., f.*)   mail carrier
casa (*f.*)   firm, company, business; house, home
— **de cambio** (*f.*)   currency exchange office
— **matriz** (*f.*)   main office
casado(a)   married
casarse (con)   to get married, to marry
casero(a)   homemade
casetera (*f.*)   VCR
casi   almost
— **crudo(a)**   almost raw; rare (*meat*)
casilla de correo (*f.*)   post office box
casita (*f.*)   little house
caso (*m.*)   case; cause
un — **perdido**   a lost cause
catálogo (*m.*)   catalogue
catedral (*f.*)   cathedral
causado(a)   caused
cebolla (*f.*)   onion
ceda el paso   yield
celebrar   to celebrate
cena (*f.*)   dinner; supper
cenar   to have supper (dinner)
cenicero (*m.*)   ashtray
centavo (*m.*)   cent, penny; cash
centímetro (*m.*)   centimeter
centro (*m.*)   downtown (area), center city
— **comercial** (*m.*)   shopping center, mall
— **de la ciudad** (*m.*)   downtown, center of the
city
cepillar(se)   to brush (oneself)
— **los dientes**   to brush one's teeth
cepillo de dientes (*m.*)   toothbrush
cerca   near

    — de aquí   near here
cercano(a)   near, close by
cereal (*m.*)   cereal
cerradura (*f.*)   lock
cerrar (e:ie)   to close
certificado de depósito (*m.*)   certificate of
   deposit (C.D.)
certificado(a)   registered
cerveza (*f.*)   beer
césped (*m.*)   lawn; grass
champaña (*m.*)   champagne
champú (*m.*)   shampoo
chapa (*f.*)   license plate
chaqueta (*f.*)   jacket
charlar   to talk, to chat
chasis (*m.*)   chassis
Chau.   Bye.
cheque (*m.*)   check
   — al portador (*m.*)   check to the bearer
   — de caja (*m.*)   cashier's check
   — de viajero (*m.*)   traveler's check
   — sin fondos (*m.*)   bounced check;
   overdrawn check
chequear   to check
chequera (*f.*)   checkbook
chícharos (*m. pl.*)   peas
chico(a) (*adj.*)   small, little
chile (*m.*)   chile (bell pepper)
chileno(a)   Chilean
chimenea (*f.*)   fireplace
chinche (*f.*)   thumbtack
chocar   to collide; to have a collision
chocolate (*m.*)   chocolate
chofer (*m., f.*)   chauffeur, driver

chuleta (*f.*) chop
cibernética (*f.*) computer science
cicatriz (*f.*) scar
cielo (*m.*) sky
ciencias económicas (*f. pl.*) economics
ciento (*m.*) hundred
cigarrillo (*m.*) cigarette
cilindro (*m.*) cylinder
cinco five
cincuenta fifty
cine (*m.*) movie theater
cintura (*f.*) waist
cinturón (*m.*) belt
   — de seguridad (*m.*) seat belt
circulación (*f.*) circulation
circular (*f.*) circular
cita (*f.*) appointment, rendezvous
ciudad (*f.*) city
ciudadano(a) (*m., f.*) citizen
claro(a) clear
  claro que sí of course
clase (*f.*) class; kind, type
cláusula (*f.*) clause
clave (*f.*) code
cliente (*m., f.*) client, customer
club automovilístico (*m.*) auto club
cobertura (*f.*) coverage
cobija (*f.*) blanket (*Méx.*)
cobrar to charge
   — o devolver (C.O.D.) collect on delivery
   (C.O.D.)
   — un cheque to cash a check
cobro (*m.*) collection (*of debts*)
coche (*m.*) car

— **cama** (*m.*)   sleeper car (Pullman)

— **comedor** (*m.*)   dining car

cocina (*f.*)   kitchen; stove

cocinar   to cook

coco (*m.*)   coconut

coctel (*m.*)   cocktail

código (*m.*)   code

codo (*m.*)   elbow

codueño(a) (*m., f.*)   co-owner

coger   to take

cojinetes (*m. pl.*)   roller bearings

cola (*f.*)   line (*of people*)

colchón (*m.*)   mattress

collar (*m.*)   necklace

colocar   to place

colocarse   to take place; to be open

colón (*m.*)   currency of Costa Rica and El
   Salvador

colonia (*f.*)   cologne

color (*m.*)   color

colorado(a)   red

comedor (*m.*)   dining room

comején (*m.*)   termite

comenzar (e:ie)   to begin, to start

comer   to eat

comercial   commercial

comida (*f.*)   food; lunch; meal

comisión (*f.*)   comission

como   since, being that; like, as

   — **siempre**   as always, as usual

¿cómo?   how?

   ¿— **es?**   What is he (she, it) like?

   ¿— **está Ud.?**   How are you?

   — **no**   certainly, of course

¿— **son?** What are (they) like?

cómoda (*f.*) chest of drawers, dresser

comodidad (*f.*) comfort, convenience

cómodo(a) comfortable

compacto(a) compact

compañero(a) (*m., f.*) classmate

— **de clase** (*m., f.*) classmate

— **de cuarto** (*m., f.*) roommate

compañía (*f.*) company

comparar to compare

compatible compatible

compensación (*f.*) compensation

compensar to compensate

competencia (*f.*) competition; athletic meet

competir (e:i) to compete

competitivo(a) competitive

completar to fill out (*a form*)

completo(a) complete; full

composición de textos (*f.*) word processing

compra (*f.*) buying; purchase

comprador(a) (*m., f.*) buyer

comprar to buy

compraventa (*f.*) purchase and sale agreement

comprender to understand

comprensivo(a) comprehensive

comprobante (*m.*) claim check; (written) proof or verification, written receipt

— **del sueldo y de los descuentos** (*m.*) wage and tax statement (W-2)

computación (*f.*) computation

computador(a) (*m., f.*) computer

— **portátil** (*m., f.*) laptop computer

comunicación (*f.*) communication

con with

¿**— cuánta anticipación?** How far in advance?

— destino a... with destination to . . .

— mucho gusto with (much) pleasure

— (su) permiso excuse me

¿**— quién?** with whom?

¿**— quién quieres hablar?** With whom would you like to speak?

— una condición on one condition

— tal que provided that

— vista a... with a view to (of) . . .

conceder un crédito to extend credit

concepto (*m.*) concept

concierto (*m.*) concert

conciliar reconcile

condado (*m.*) county

condición (*f.*) condition

— de costumbre en la plaza (*f.*) usual terms in the market

— de pago (*f.*) term of payment

condominio (*m.*) condominium

conducir to drive

conductor(a) (*m., f.*) driver

conectar to connect

confeccionar to make, to prepare, to put together

confirmar to confirm

congelado(a) frozen

conjunto (*m.*) outfit

— de pantalón y chaqueta (*m.*) pantsuit

conjunto(a) joint

conmigo with me

conocer to know; to be acquainted, to be familiar with

conocido(a) known
conseguir (e:i) to get, to obtain
consejero(a) (*m., f.*) adviser
consejo (*m.*) advice
consignatario(a) (*m., f.*) consignee
consistir (en) to consist (of)
constancia (*f.*) proof
construido(a) built
  — a la orden custom built
consulta (*f.*) consultation
consultar to consult
consultorio (*m.*) doctor's office
consumidor(a) (*m., f.*) consumer
consumir to consume
contabilidad (*f.*) accounting
contable accounting
contador(a) (*m., f.*) accountant
  — público(a) titulado(a) (*m., f.*) Certified
    Public Accountant (C.P.A.)
contar (o:ue) to count
  — con to have available
contenedor (*m.*) container
contener to contain
contestación pagada (*f.*) prepaid response
continuar to continue
contra against
contratar to hire; to employ
contrato (*m.*) contract
contribución (*f.*) contribution; (real estate) tax
contribuir to contribute
contribuyente (*m., f.*) taxpayer
conveniente convenient
convenir to suit, to be good for, to be advisable
  — en to agree on

convenirle a uno   to be to one's advantage
conversación (*f.*)   conversation
conversar   to talk, to converse
convertirse (e:ie) (en)   to turn into, to become
cooperación (*f.*)   cooperation
copa (*f.*)   glass; wine glass
copia (*f.*)   copy
corazón (*m.*)   heart
corbata (*f.*)   tie
corbina (*f.*)   sea bass
cordero (*m.*)   lamb
cordialmente   cordially
córdoba (*m.*)   currency of Nicaragua
corredor(a) de bienes raíces (*m., f.*)   real estate
   agent
correo (*m.*)   mail, post office
   — **aéreo** (*m.*)   air mail
   — **electrónico** (*m.*)   electronic mail (e-mail)
correr   to run
   — **con**   to be in charge of
correspondencia (*f.*)   mail; correspondence
   — **comercial** (*f.*)   business correspondence
corriente   current
cortar   to cut
   —**se el pelo**   to get a haircut
cortina (*f.*)   curtain
corto(a)   short
cosa (*f.*)   thing
costar (o:ue)   to cost
coste (*m.*)   cost
   —**, seguro y flete (C.S.F.)**   cost, insurance,
      and freight (C.I.F.)
costoso(a)   costly
creación (*f.*)   creation

crecer to grow
crédito (*m.*) credit
creer to believe, to think
crema (*f.*) cream
   — de afeitar (*f.*) shaving cream
Creo que sí. I think so.
criada (*f.*) maid
criarse to be raised
crudo(a) raw; rare (*meat*)
cruzar to cross
cuadra (*f.*) block
cuadrado(a) square
cuadrar to reconcile
cuadro (*m.*) painting
cual which, what
¿cuál? which?; what?
¿cuáles? which (ones)? (*pl.*)
cualquier cosa anything
cualquier(a) any
cuando when
¿cuándo? when?
¿cuánto(a)? how much?
   ¿Cuánto es? How much is it?
   ¿Cuánto mide Ud.? How tall are you?
   ¿Cuánto tiempo? How long?
¿cuántos(as)? how many?
cuarenta forty
cuarto (*m.*) room
   — de baño (*m.*) bathroom
   — de lavar (*m.*) laundry room
   — para huéspedes (*m.*) guest room
   — principal (*m.*) master bedroom
cuarto(a) fourth
cúbico(a) cubic

cubierto(a)   covered
cubrir   to cover
cuchara (*f.*)   spoon
cucharada (*f.*)   spoonful
cucharadita (*f.*)   teaspoonful
cuchillo (*m.*)   knife
cuello (*m.*)   neck
cuenta (*f.*)   account; bill; check
   — **a cobrar** (*f.*)   account receivable
   — **a pagar** (*f.*)   account payable
   — **acreedora** (*f.*)   credit account
   — **conjunta** (*f.*)   joint account
   — **corriente** (*f.*)   checking account
   — **de ahorros** (*f.*)   savings account
   — **de cheques** (*f.*)   checking account (*Méx.*)
   — **del mercado de dinero** (*f.*)   money market account
   — **deudora** (*f.*)   debit account
   — **individual de retiro** (*f.*)   individual retirement account (I.R.A.)
cuero (*m.*)   leather
cuerpo (*m.*)   body
cuidado (*m.*)   care, caution
cuidado(a)   cared for; kept
cuidadosamente   carefully
cuidar   to take care of
   — **la línea**   to watch one's figure
culpa (*f.*)   blame, guilt
culpable   at fault, guilty
cultura (*f.*)   culture
cumpleaños (*m.*)   birthday
cuota inicial (*f.*)   down payment
curso (*m.*)   course
curva (*f.*)   curve

D

dama (*f.*) lady
danza aeróbica (*f.*) aerobic dance
daño (*m.*) damage
dar to give
   — a la calle to overlook the street
datos (*m. pl.*) information; data
de from, of, about
   — acuerdo (con) in accordance (with)
   — cambios mecánicos standard shift (car)
   — costumbre usual
   — estatura mediana (of) medium height
   — ida one way
   — ida y vuelta round trip
   — la izquierda (derecha) to the left (right)
   — modo que so (that)
   — nada. You're welcome. (It's nothing.)
   — niño(a) as a child
   — nuevo again
   — primera (calidad) top quality
   — todos modos anyway, in any case
   — un lugar a otro from one place to another
   — uso used
   — vestir dressy
debajo (de) under, underneath
debe (*m.*) debit
deber must, should, to have to; to owe
debido(a) due
débil weak
debitar to debit
decidir to decide
decímetro (*m.*) decimeter
decir (e:i) to say, to tell

   — **algo en broma**   to joke, to kid
   — **que sí (no)**   to say yes (no)
declaración (*f.*)   declaration
   — **de aduana** (*f.*)   customs form
   — **de impuestos** (*f.*)   tax return
declarar   to declare; to depose
   — **culpable**   to declare at fault
   —**se en quiebra**   to declare bankruptcy
dedo (*m.*)   finger
   — **del pie** (*m.*)   toe
deducción (*f.*)   deduction
   — **general** (*f.*)   standard deduction
deducible   deductible
deducir   to deduct
defensa (*f.*)   bumper
dejar   to leave (behind); to let, to allow
   — **de (+ *inf.*)**   to stop (doing something)
   — **de ser**   to be no longer
   se lo puedo — en...   I can give it to you for. . .
deleitarse   to delight in
delgado(a)   thin, slim
delicioso(a)   delicious
delito (*m.*)   crime, offense
   — **mayor (grave)** (*m.*)   felony
   — **menor (menos grave)** (*m.*)   misdemeanor
demanda (*f.*)   lawsuit
demandado(a) (*m., f.*)   defendant (civil case)
demandar   to file a lawsuit, to sue
demasiado (*adv.*)   too much, too
demasiado(a) (*adj.*)   too, too much
demora (*f.*)   delay
demorar   to take (*time*); to last (*a length of time*)
demostración (*f.*)   show
dentro de   in, within

denunciar to report (*a crime*)
departamento (*m.*) apartment; department
depender (de) to depend (on)
dependiente (*m., f.*) dependent
deporte (*m.*) sport
depositante (*m., f.*) depositor
depositar to deposit
depositario(a) depositary; receiver
depósito (*m.*) deposit
derecha (*f.*) right (direction)
derecho (*adv.*) straight
   siga — go straight ahead
derecho(a) right
derechos (*m. pl.*) (customs) duty
derrota (*f.*) defeat
desaparecer to disappear
desastre (*m.*) disaster
desayunar to have breakfast
desayuno (*m.*) breakfast
descafeinado(a) decaffeinated
descansar to rest
descarga (*f.*) unloading
descargar to unload
descartar to rule out
descomponerse to break down
descompuesto(a) broken (down), out of order
desconocido(a) (*m., f.*) stranger
descontar (o:ue) to give a discount of
describir to describe
descripción del contenido de trabajo (*f.*) job
   description
descuento (*m.*) discount, deduction, reduction
desde from, since
   — luego of course

— **que** since
desear to want, to wish
desempeñar to hold; to carry out
desempleo (*m.*) unemployment
desgraciadamente unfortunately
desinfectar to disinfect
desinflado(a) flat
desocupado(a) vacant, empty
desocupar to check out, to vacate
— **la habitación** to check out; to vacate a
room
desodorante (*m.*) deodorant
despacho de boletos (*m.*) ticket office
despacio slow, slowly
despedida (*f.*) farewell; closing
despegar to take off (*a plane*)
despegue (*m.*) takeoff
despertar(se) (e:ie) to wake up
después (de) later; afterwards
destinatario(a) (*m., f.*) addressee; recipient
destino (*m.*) destination
desvío (*m.*) detour
detallista (*m., f.*) retailer
detergente (*m.*) detergent
detrás de behind
deuda (*f.*) debt
deudor(a) (*m., f.*) debtor
devolver (o:ue) to return, to give back
día (*m.*) day
— **de semana** (*m.*) weekday
— **de trabajo** (*m.*) workday
— **del santo** (*m.*) saint's day
— **hábil** (*m.*) weekday
— **laborante** (*m.*) workday

diabetes (*f.*)   diabetes
diabético(a)   diabetic
diamante (*m.*)   diamond
diariamente   daily
diario (*m.*)   newspaper
diario(a)   daily
diarrea (*f.*)   diarrhea
dibujo (*m.*)   drawing; design
diciembre   December
diecinueve   nineteen
diente (*m.*)   tooth
dieta (*f.*)   diet
dietista (*m., f.*)   dietician
diez   ten
diferencia (*f.*)   difference
difícil   difficult
dificultad (*f.*)   difficulty
digo   I mean
dinero (*m.*)   money
   — **en efectivo** (*m.*)   cash
dirección (*f.*)   address
   — **anterior** (*f.*)   previous address
directamente   directly
directo(a)   direct
directorio telefónico (*m.*)   phone book
disco (*m.*)   record
   — **de programación** (*m.*)   computer disk(ette)
   — **duro** (*m.*)   hard drive
   — **flexible** (*m.*)   floppy disk drive
discoteca (*f.*)   discotheque
discutir   to discuss
diseñado(a)   designed
diseñar   to design
diseño (*m.*)   design

disminución (*f.*)   decrease
disponerse   to set (*in place*)
disponible   available
disposición (*f.*)   regulation
disquete (*m.*)   computer disk(ette)
distinto(a)   different
distribuir   to distribute
divertido(a)   fun, amusing
divertirse (e:ie)   to have fun, to have a good time
dividendo (*m.*)   dividend
divorciado(a)   divorced
doblar   to turn; to fold
doble (*m.*)   double; twice
doce   twelve
docena (*f.*)   dozen
doctor(a) (*m., f.*)   doctor, M.D.
documento (*m.*)   document
   — mercantil (*m.*)   business document
dólar (*m.*)   dollar
doler (o:ue)   to hurt, to ache, to feel pain
dolor (*m.*)   pain
   — de garganta (*m.*)   sore throat
domicilio (*m.*)   address
donación (*f.*)   donation
donar   to donate
donde   where
¿dónde?   where?
dormir (o:ue)   to sleep
dormitorio (*m.*)   bedroom
dos   two
droga (*f.*)   drug
ducha (*f.*)   shower
ducharse   to shower
dudar   to doubt

dueño(a) (*m., f.*)   owner
dulce (*m.*)   sweet, confection
dulcería (*f.*)   candy store
durante   during
durar   to last
durazno (*m.*)   peach

E

echar   to drop
  — al correo   to mail
económico(a)   economic(al)
edad (*f.*)   age
edición (*f.*)   edition; issue
edificio (*m.*)   building
  — de apartamentos (*m.*)   apartment building
efectivo (*m.*)   cash
efectivo(a)   effective
efectuarse   to take place
eficiente   efficient
egreso (*m.*)   expenditure
ejemplar (*m.*)   copy; sample
ejercicio (*m.*)   exercise
el mes que viene (*m.*)   next month, the coming
  month
él (*m.*)   he
electricidad (*f.*)   electricity
eléctrico(a)   electric
electrodoméstico (*m.*)   appliance
elegante   elegant
elegir (e:i)   to choose, to select
elevador (*m.*)   elevator
eliminar   to eliminate
ella (*f.*)   she

ellos(as) (*m., f.*)   they
embalaje (*m.*)   packing
embarazada   pregnant
emergencia (*f.*)   emergency
empanizado(a)   breaded
empatar   to tie (*the score*)
empezar (e:ie)   to begin, to start
empleado(a) (*m., f.*)   employee, clerk
 — **de cuello blanco** (*m., f.*)   white collar
   worker
empleador(a) (*m., f.*)   employer
empleo (*m.*)   employment, job
empresa (*f.*)   enterprise, company
en   on; in; at
 — **blanco y negro**   in black and white
 — **casa**   at home
 — **caso de que**   in case
 — **colores**   in color
 — **cuanto**   as soon as
 — **cuanto a**   in regard to
 — **efectivo**   in cash
 — **exceso (de)**   in excess (of)
 — **existencia**   in stock
 — **fondo (depósito)**   (in) deposit
 — **mi nombre**   in my name
 — **punto**   sharp, on the dot (*time*)
 ¿— **qué puedo (podemos) servirle?**   How
   may I (we) help you?
 — **realidad**   indeed
 — **regla**   in order
 — **seguida**   right away
 — **seguida va para allá.**   He's on his way
   there.
 — **total**   in all

enamorado(a) in love
encabezamiento (*m.*) heading
encantarle a uno to love
encargado(a) (*m., f.*) manager, person in charge
encargar to entrust
 —se (de) to take charge (of); to see after
encendido(a) turned on (*electricity*), lit up
enchufar to plug in
enchufe (*m.*) electrical outlet; socket
encontrar (o:ue) to find; to meet
encuesta (*f.*) poll; survey
enero January
enfadado(a) angry
enfermedad (*f.*) disease, sickness
enfermero(a) (*m., f.*) nurse
enfermo(a) sick
enganche (*m.*) down payment (*Méx.*)
engordar to gain weight
engrase (*m.*) lubrication, lube and oil change
enojado(a) angry
ensalada (*f.*) salad
enseñar to show, to teach
enseres (*m. pl.*) fixtures
entender (e:ie) to understand
entonces then, in that case
entrada (*f.*) arrival; entry; down payment
 — ilegal (*f.*) trespassing
entrar to enter, to go in
entre between
entrega especial (*f.*) special delivery
entregar to deliver
entremés (*m.*) appetizer
entrepaño (*m.*) shelf
entrevista (*f.*) interview

enviar   to send
envolver (o:ue)   to wrap
   — **para regalo**   to gift-wrap
envuelto(a)   wrapped
enyesar   to put in a cast
época (*f.*)   time
equipaje (*m.*)   baggage, luggage
equipo (*m.*)   team; equipment
   — **de computación** (*m.*)   computer hardware
   — **electrónico** (*m.*)   electronic device
equitativo(a)   fair, reasonable
equivalente   equivalent
error (*m.*)   error
es decir   that is to say, in other words
Es verdad.   It's true.
escala (*f.*)   stopover
   — **de impuestos** (*f.*)   tax rate table
escalar   to climb
escalera (*f.*)   stair
   — **de mano** (*f.*)   ladder
   — **mecánica** (*f.*)   escalator
   — **rodante** (*f.*)   escalator
escáner (*m.*)   scanner
escanógrafo (*m.*)   scanner
escaparate (*m.*)   shop window, display window
escoba (*f.*)   broom
escoger   to choose, to select
escribir   to write
escritorio (*m.*)   desk
escritura (*f.*)   deed
escuchar   to listen (to)
escuela (*f.*)   school
eso   that
   — **es todo.**   That's all.

— **incluye...** That includes . . .

espacio (*m.*) commercial space

espalda (*f.*) back

España Spain

español (*m.*) Spanish (language)

español(a) (*m., f.*) Spaniard; (*adj.*) Spanish

especial special

especialidad (*f.*) specialty

especialista (*m., f.*) specialist

especialización (*f.*) major, specialization

espejo (*m.*) mirror

espejuelos (*m. pl.*) eyeglasses

esperar to wait (for); to expect; to hope

espinaca (*f.*) spinach

esposo(a) (*m., f.*) husband, wife

esquiar to ski

esquina (*f.*) corner

— **superior derecha (izquierda)** (*f.*) upper
right (left) corner

esta noche tonight

esta vez this time

estable stable

establecimiento (*m.*) establishment; shop

— **comercial** (*m.*) business

estación (*f.*) station; season

— **de servicio** (*f.*) service station

— **de trenes** (*f.*) railroad station

estacionamiento (*m.*) parking; parking lot

estacionar to park (*a car*)

estadística (*f.*) statistics

estado (*m.*) state

— **civil** (*m.*) marital status

— **de cuenta** (*m.*) statement of account

— **de pérdidas y ganancias** (*m.*) profit and loss statement

— **financiero** (*m.*) financial statement

Estados Unidos (*m. pl.*) United States

estampilla (*f.*) (postage) stamp

estante (*m.*) shelf

estar to be

— **a (su) disposición** to be at (your) disposal

— **bien si...** (to be) all right if . . .

— **de acuerdo** to agree

— **de moda** to be in style

— **de vacaciones** to be on vacation

— **dispuesto(a) a** to be willing (to)

— **seguro(a)** to be sure, certain

estatura (*f.*) height

este (*m.*) east

este(a) this

estimado (*m.*) estimate

estofado(a) stewed

estómago (*m.*) stomach

estos(as) these

estructura (*f.*) structure

estuco (*m.*) stucco

estudiante (*m., f.*) student

estudiar to study

estupendo(a) great, fantastic

etiqueta (*f.*) label

evaluar to evaluate, to assess

evasión fiscal (*f.*) tax evasion

eventualidad (*f.*) eventuality

evitar to avoid

exactamente exactly

exagerar to exaggerate

examen (*m.*)   exam, examination, test
  — **parcial (de mitad de curso)** (*m.*)   midterm
    exam
exceder   to exceed
excepto   except
exceso (*m.*)   excess
  — **de equipaje** (*m.*)   excess luggage
  — **de velocidad** (*m.*)   speeding
exclusión (*f.*)   exclusion
exclusivamente   exclusively
exclusivo(a)   exclusive
excursión (*f.*)   excursion, tour
excusado (*m.*)   bathroom (toilet) (*Méx.*)
exención (*f.*)   exemption
exigir   to require; to demand
éxito (*m.*)   success
experiencia (*f.*)   experience
experto(a) (*m., f.*)   expert witness
explicar   to explain
exportación (*f.*)   export
exportar   to export
expresión (*f.*)   expression
expreso (*m.*)   express (train)
expreso(a)   express
expulsar   to expel
exquisito(a)   exquisite
extender (e:ie) un cheque   to write a check
exterior (*m.*)   exterior
extinguidor de incendios (*m.*)   fire
    extinguisher
extorsión (*f.*)   extortion
extra   extra
extraer   to extract
extranjero(a) (*m., f.*)   foreigner

F

fabricación (*f.*) manufacture
fabricado(a) manufactured
fachada (*f.*) facade
fácil easy
fácilmente easily
facsímil(e) (*m.*) facsimile, fax
falda (*f.*) skirt
fallecer to die
faltar to be lacking
familia (*f.*) family
familiares (*m. pl.*) relatives
fantástico(a) fantastic
farmacia (*f.*) drugstore, pharmacy
farol (*m.*) light
favor de (+ *inf.*) please (do something)
fax (*m.*) facsimile, fax
febrero February
fecha (*f.*) date
   — de cierre (*f.*) closing date
   — de vencimiento (*f.*) expiration date, due
     date
   — fija (*f.*) by a certain date
federal federal
felicidades (*f. pl.*) congratulations
feliz happy
fenómeno natural (*m.*) natural phenomenon,
  act of God
feo(a) ugly, bad-looking
ferretería (*f.*) hardware store
ferrocarril (*m.*) railroad; train
fibra (*f.*) fiber
ficha (*f.*) token

fideos (*m. pl.*)   noodles
fiebre (*f.*)   fever
fiesta (*f.*)   party
 — de cumpleaños (*f.*)   birthday party
figurarse   to imagine
fijo(a)   fixed
fila (*f.*)   row, line
filmar   to film
filme (*m.*)   film
fin (*m.*)   end
 — de semana (*m.*)   weekend
final   final
financiamiento (*m.*)   financing
financiero(a)   financial
firma (*f.*)   firm, company, business; signing, signature
firmar   to sign
fiscal (*m., f.*)   district attorney
física (*f.*)   physics
flan (*m.*)   custard
flete (*m.*)   freight
florería (*f.*)   flower shop
folio (*m.*)   folio (page) (*i.e., in accounting books*)
folleto (*m.*)   booklet
fondo mutuo (*m.*)   mutual fund
fondos (*m. pl.*)   funds; deposits
forma (*f.*)   form
 — de pago (*f.*)   means of payment
foto (*f.*)   photo
fotocopiadora (*f.*)   photocopier
fotografía (*f.*)   photography, photograph
fractura (*f.*)   fracture
fracturar(se)   to fracture
frágil   fragile

francés(a)   French
franco a bordo   free on board (F.O.B.)
franqueo (*m.*)   postage
fraude (*m.*)   fraud
frazada (*f.*)   blanket
fregadero (*m.*)   kitchen sink
fregar (e:ie)   to wash, to scrub
freír (e:i)   to fry
freno (*m.*)   brake
frente (*f.*)   forehead
  — a   in front of
fresa (*f.*)   strawberry
fresco(a)   fresh
frijol (*m.*)   bean
frío(a)   cold
frito(a)   fried
frontera (*f.*)   border; frontier
fruta (*f.*)   fruit
frutería (*f.*)   fruit store
fuego (*m.*)   fire
fuerte   strong
fuerza mayor (*f.*)   natural phenomenon, act of
  God
fumador(a) (*m., f.*)   smoker
fumar   to smoke
funcionar   to work, to function
funda (*f.*)   pillowcase
fútbol (*m.*)   soccer; football
futuro (*m.*)   future

G

gabinete (*m.*)   cabinet

gafas (*f. pl.*)   eyeglasses
— **de sol** (*f. pl.*)   sunglasses
galleta (*f.*)   cracker; cookie
galletica (*f.*)   cookie
galletita (*f.*)   cookie
gamba (*f.*)   shrimp (*España*)
ganador(a) (*m., f.*)   winner
ganancia (*f.*)   profit; earnings
ganar   to earn; to win
garaje (*m.*)   garage
garantía (*f.*)   guarantee
garganta (*f.*)   throat
gaseosa (*f.*)   soda pop, soft drink
gasolina (*f.*)   gasoline
— **sin plomo** (*f.*)   unleaded gasoline
gasolinera (*f.*)   service station
gastar   to spend (*money*); to use (*resources*)
gastos (*m. pl.*)   expenses; costs
— **de cierre** (*m. pl.*)   closing costs
— **de representación** (*m. pl.*)   entertainment expenses
— **generales** (*m. pl.*)   overhead expenses
— **varios** (*m. pl.*)   sundry expenses
gato (*m.*)   jack
gelatina (*f.*)   gelatine
generación (*f.*)   generation
general   general
genérico(a)   generic
géneros (*m. pl.*)   goods
gente (*f.*)   people
gerente (*m., f.*)   administrator, director, manager
— **general** (*m., f.*)   general manager
gestión (*f.*)   work or actions someone has to do or has done

gimnasio (*m.*)   gymnasium

girado(a)   drawn; (*m., f.*) party that will pay the amount indicated (bill of exchange)

girador(a) (*m, f*)   party that orders payment of a determined amount (bill of exchange)

girar un cheque   to write a check

giro (*m.*)   line of business

— **postal** (*m.*)   money order

— **telegráfico** (*m.*)   moneygram

gobierno (*m.*)   government

golpear(se)   to hit (oneself)

goma (*f.*)   tire; rubber band (*Puerto Rico*)

— **pinchada** (*f.*)   flat tire

gordo(a)   fat

grabadora (*f.*)   tape recorder

— **de video** (*f.*)   VCR

gracias   thank you

muchas —   thank you very much

graduación (*f.*)   graduation

graduarse   to graduate

gráfico (*m.*)   graphic

grande   big, large

grandes almacenes (*m. pl.*)   department store

grapa (*f.*)   staple

grapadora (*f.*)   stapler

grasa (*f.*)   fat

gratis (*adv.*)   free

grave   serious

gris   grey

gritar   to shout, to scream

grúa (*f.*)   tow truck

guachinango (*m.*)   red snapper (*Méx.*)

guajolote (*m.*)   turkey (*Méx.*)

guanajo (*m.*)   turkey (*Cuba*)

guapo(a) handsome, beautiful
guaraní (*m.*) currency of Paraguay
guardabarros (*m.*) fender
guardafangos (*m.*) fender
guía (*f.*) consignment note (*trucking*)
   — de teléfonos (*f.*) phone book
   — para turistas (*f.*) tourist guide
guiar to drive (*Puerto Rico*)
guisado (*m.*) stew
guisado(a) stewed
guisantes (*m. pl.*) peas
guiso (*m.*) stew
gustar to like, to be pleasing (to)

H

haber (*m.*) credit
habitación (*f.*) room
habitado(a) occupied (*i.e., a house*)
hábito (*m.*) habit
hablar to speak, to talk
hacer to do, to make
   — bien to do the right thing
   — caso to pay attention
   — cola to stand in line
   — (unas) compras to do (some) shopping
   — ejercicio to exercise
   — escala to make a stopover
   — falta to need, to lack
   — juego to match
   — la cama to make the bed
   — planes to make plans
   — resaltar to emphasize
   — reservaciones to make reservations

    — **un pedido** to place an order

    — **una radiografía** to take an X-ray

    —**le bien a uno** to do one (some) good

hacia to, toward

hambre (*f.*) hunger

hamburguesa (*f.*) hamburger

harina (*f.*) flour

hasta until; up to

    — **llegar** until you arrive

    — **llegar a** up to, until one hits

    — **luego.** I'll see you later.

    — **mañana.** See you tomorrow.

    — **que** until

hay there is, there are

    — **de todo** there are all kinds of things

    — **que (+ *inf.*)** it is necessary (to do something)

hecho(a) a la orden custom built

helado (*m.*) ice cream

heredero(a) (*m., f.*) heir

herencia (*f.*) inheritance

herida (*f.*) wound

hermano (hno.) (*m.*) brother

hermoso(a) beautiful

hervido(a) boiled

hervir (e:ie) to boil

higiénico(a) hygienic

hijo(a) (*m., f.*) son; daughter

hijos (*m. pl.*) children

hipermercado (*m.*) supermarket

hipoteca (*f.*) mortgage

Hizo bien. You did the right thing.

hogar (*m.*) home

hoja de análisis (de cálculo) (*f.*) spread sheet

Hola. Hello., Hi.
hombre (*m.*)   man
hombro (*m.*)   shoulder
homicidio no premeditado (*m.*)   manslaughter
hondo(a)   deep
honorario (*m.*)   fee
hora (*f.*)   hour
horario (*m.*)   schedule, timetable
horneado(a)   baked
horno (*m.*)   oven
horóscopo (*m.*)   horoscope
hospital (*m.*)   hospital
hotel (*m.*)   hotel
hoy   today
  — mismo   this very day
¿Hubo heridos?   Was anybody hurt?
huésped (*m., f.*)   guest
huevo (*m.*)   egg
  — duro (*m.*)   hard-boiled egg
humano(a)   human
humo (*m.*)   smoke
hundido(a)   sunken
huracán (*m.*)   hurricane

I

idea (*f.*)   idea
identificación (*f.*)   identification; I.D.
idioma (*m.*)   language
iglesia (*f.*)   church
igual (que)   equal to, the same as
iguala (*f.*)   arrangement (*Cuba*)
importado(a)   imported
importador(a) (*m., f.*)   importer

importante   important
importar   to import; to matter
importe (*m.*)   amount, price
impresión (*f.*)   printing
impreso (*m.*)   printed matter
impresor(a) (*m., f.*)   printer
imprimir   to print
impuesto (*m.*)   (customs) duty; tax
   — **a la propiedad** (*m.*)   property tax
   — **al valor agregado (I.V.A.)** (*m.*)   value-
   added tax (VAT)
   — **estatal (del estado)** (*m.*)   state tax
   — **sobre la venta** (*m.*)   sales tax
incendio (*m.*)   fire
   — **premeditado** (*m.*)   arson
incluido(a)   included
incluir   to include
incómodo(a)   uncomfortable
inconveniente (*m.*)   inconvenience
indemnización (*f.*)   compensation;
   indemnification
indicación (*f.*)   specification
indicar   to indicate
individual   individual
industria (*f.*)   industry
infección (*f.*)   infection
influencia (*f.*)   influence
información (*f.*)   information
informática (*f.*)   computer science
informe (*m.*)   report; (*pl.*) information
ingeniero(a) (*m., f.*)   engineer
inglés (*m.*)   English (language)
ingreso (*m.*)   income
   — **ajustado bruto** (*m.*)   adjusted gross income

— **ajustado neto** (*m.*)   adjusted net income
— **(en) bruto** (*m.*)   gross income
— **sujeto a impuestos** (*m.*)   taxable income
inicial (*adj.*) initial; (*f.*) initial
inmigración (*f.*)   immigration
inmovilizado(a)   tied up; locked
inmuebles (*m. pl.*)   real estate; buildings
innecesario(a)   unnecessary
inocente   not guilty
inodoro (*m.*)   toilet
inquilino(a) (*m., f.*)   renter
insolvencia (*f.*)   bankruptcy, insolvency
insolvente   insolvent
inspección (*f.*)   inspection
inspeccionar   to inspect
inspector(a) (*m., f.*)   inspector
instalado(a)   installed; available
instantáneo(a)   instant
institución (*f.*)   institution
instrumento (*m.*)   instrument
— **de crédito** (*m.*)   credit document
inteligente   intelligent
intercomunicador (*m.*)   intercom
interés (*m.*)   interest
— **compuesto** (*m.*)   compound interest
interesado(a)   interested
interesar   to interest
interior   interior
internacional   international
Internet (*f.*)   Internet
intérprete (*m., f.*)   interpreter
intersección (*f.*)   intersection
intestado(a)   intestate
introducción de datos (*f.*)   data entry

introducir to introduce
inundación (*f.*) flood
inútilmente uselessly
invalidez (*f.*) disability; disablement
inventario (*m.*) inventory
inversión (*f.*) investment
invertido(a) invested
invertir (e:ie) to invest
investigar to investigate
invierno (*m.*) winter
invitación (*f.*) invitation
invitado(a) (*m., f.*) guest
invitar to invite
inyección (*f.*) shot
  — **antitetánica** (*f.*) tetanus shot
ir to go
  — **a (+ *inf.*)** to be going to (do something)
  — **de caza** to go hunting
  — **de compras** to go shopping
  — **de excursión** to go on a tour
  — **de pesca** to go fishing
  — **de picnic** to go on a picnic
  — **por su cuenta** to be paid by you, on one's
    account
  — **zigzagueando** to weave (*car*)
irle bien a uno to do well
itinerario (*m.*) schedule, timetable, itinerary
izquierda (*f.*) left

J

¡Ja! Ha!
jabón (*m.*) soap
jalea (*f.*) jam

jarabe (*m.*) syrup
— **para la tos** (*m.*) cough syrup
jardín (*m.*) garden
jarra (*f.*) pitcher
jefe(a) (*m., f.*) boss
— **de compras** (*m., f.*) purchasing manager
— **de familia** (*m., f.*) head of household
— **de ventas** (*m., f.*) sales manager
jornal (*m.*) daily wage(s)
joven (*adj.*) young; (*m., f.*) young man, young woman
joyería (*f.*) jewelry store
jubilación (*f.*) retirement
juego de cuarto (dormitorio) (*m.*) bedroom set
jueves (*m.*) Thursday
juez (*m., f.*) judge
jugar (u:ue) to play
jugo (*m.*) juice
— **de naranja** (*m.*) orange juice
— **de tomate** (*m.*) tomato juice
juguetería (*f.*) toy shop
juicio (*m.*) trial
julio July
junio June
junta (*f.*) meeting
juntos(as) together
jurado (*m.*) jury

K

kilo (*m.*) kilo
kilogramo (*m.*) kilo, kilogram
kilómetro (*m.*) kilometer
kiosco (*m.*) kiosk, magazine stand

L

laboratorio de lenguas (*m.*)   language laboratory

lado (*m.*)   side

ladrillo (*m.*)   brick

ladrón(ona) (*m., f.*)   thief, robber

lago (*m.*)   lake

lamentar   to be sorry for, to regret

lámpara (*f.*)   lamp

lana (*f.*)   wool

langosta (*f.*)   lobster

lápiz (*m.*)   pencil

largo (*m.*)   length

largo(a)   long

   larga distancia (*f.*)   long distance

lástima (*f.*)   pity

lastimar(se)   to get hurt

lata de la basura (*f.*)   trash can

Latinoamérica   Latin America

latinoamericano(a)   Latin American

lavabo (*m.*)   bathroom sink

lavado (*m.*)   shampoo

lavadora (*f.*)   washing machine

   — de platos (*f.*)   dishwasher

lavandería (*f.*)   laundry

lavaplatos (*m.*)   dishwasher

lavar(se)   to wash (oneself)

   — en seco   to dry-clean

leche (*f.*)   milk

lechería (*f.*)   dairy store

lechón (*m.*)   suckling pig

lechuga (*f.*)   lettuce

leer   to read

legado (*m.*)   bequest
legal   legal
lejía (*f.*)   bleach
lejos   far (away)
   — **de aquí**   far (away) from here
lema (*m.*)   slogan
lempira (*m.*)   currency of Honduras
lengua (*f.*)   tongue; language
lenguado (*m.*)   sole
lentes (*m. pl.*)   eyeglasses
lesión (*f.*)   injury
letra de molde (*f.*)   print; printing
letra de cambio (*f.*)   bill of exchange
levantar   to raise
   — **pesas**   to lift weights
   —**se**   to get up
ley (*f.*)   law
   — **de tránsito (tráfico)** (*f.*)   traffic law
libra (*f.*)   pound
libre   available, vacant, free
   — **a bordo (L.A.B.)**   free on board (F.O.B.)
   — **de derechos (impuestos)**   duty-free
libro (*m.*)   book
   — **de actas** (*m.*)   minutes book
   — **de caja** (*m.*)   cash book
   — **de ventas** (*m.*)   sales book
   — **diario** (*m.*)   journal
   — **mayor** (*m.*)   general ledger
licencia (*f.*)   license
   — **para conducir (manejar)** (*f.*)   driver's
     license
liga (*f.*)   rubber band (*Méx. y Cuba*)
límite (*m.*)   limit
limón (*m.*)   lemon

limonada (*f.*)   lemonade
limpiaparabrisas (*m.*)   windshield wiper
limpiar   to clean
— **en seco**   to dry-clean
limpieza (*f.*)   cleaning
limpio(a)   clean
lindo(a)   pretty, beautiful
línea (*f.*)   line
linóleo (*m.*)   linoleum
liquidar   to liquidate; to pay off
liquidez (*f.*)   liquidity
líquido (*m.*)   liquid
— **de frenos** (*m.*)   brake fluid
— **de la transmisión** (*m.*)   transmission fluid
lista (*f.*)   list
listo(a)   ready
litera (*f.*)   berth
— **alta** (*f.*)   upper berth
— **baja** (*f.*)   lower berth
literatura (*f.*)   literature
llamada (*f.*)   call
llamar   to call
— **por teléfono**   to call on the phone
llanta (*f.*)   tire
llave (*f.*)   key
llegar   to arrive; to become
— **a un arreglo**   to make a deal, to reach an
agreement
— **tarde (temprano)**   to be late (early)
llenar   to fill (out)
lleno(a)   full
llevar   to take (someone or something someplace);
to carry
— **a alguien**   to give someone a ride

    — **la contabilidad**   to keep the books
    — **puesto(a)**   to wear
    —**se**   to take away
llover (o:ue)   to rain
lluvia (*f.*)   rain
lo   it
    — **importante**   the important thing(s)
    — **mejor**   the best thing
    — **necesario**   the necessary thing(s)
    — **que**   what, that, which
    — **siento.**   I'm sorry.
    — **único**   the only thing
local (*adj.*)   local; commercial space
loco(a)   crazy
logo(grama) (*m.*)   logo
los (las)   the
    — **de**   those
    — **demás**   the rest, the others
    — **nuestros(as)**   ours
losa (*f.*)   tile
lubricación (*f.*)   lubrication
luego   later, then
lugar (*m.*)   place
    — **de interés** (*m.*)   place of interest
    — **de nacimiento** (*m.*)   place of birth
luna de miel (*f.*)   honeymoon
lunes (*m.*)   Monday
luz (*f.*)   light

M

madera (*f.*)   wood
madre (*f.*)   mother
maduro(a)   ripe

magnífico(a) magnificent, great

maleta (*f.*) suitcase

maletero(a) (*m., f.*) trunk; porter, skycap

maletín de mano (*m.*) handbag, carry-on bag

malo(a) bad

mamá (*f.*) mom, mother

manchado(a) stained

mandar to send

manejar to drive, to operate

   — **bajo los efectos del alcohol** driving while intoxicated

   — **con cuidado** to drive carefully

maní (*m.*) peanut

mano (*f.*) hand

   — **de obra** (*f.*) labor

manta (*f.*) blanket

mantel (*m.*) tablecloth

mantener to maintain, to keep

mantenimiento adecuado (*m.*) adequate maintenance

mantequilla (*f.*) butter

manufacturero(a) manufacturing

manzana (*f.*) apple

mañana (*f.*) morning; (*adv.*) tomorrow

mapa (*m.*) map

maquillaje (*m.*) makeup

máquina (*f.*) machine; car (*Cuba*)

   — **contestadora** (*f.*) answering machine

   — **copiadora** (*f.*) copying machine

   — **de afeitar** (*f.*) razor, shaver

   — **de escribir** (*f.*) typewriter

maquinaria (*f.*) hardware

maravilloso(a) marvelous

marca (*f.*) brand

— **de fábrica** (*f.*)   manufacturer's trade mark
— **registrada** (*f.*)   registered brand, trade mark
marcado(a)   marked
marcar   to dial; to mark; to indicate
mareado(a)   dizzy, airsick, seasick
mareo(a)   dizziness, airsickness, seasickness
margarina (*f.*)   margarine
marisco (*m.*)   shellfish; (*pl.*) seafood
marrón   brown
martes (*m.*)   Tuesday
marzo   March
más   more, plus, further
— **o menos**   more or less, approximately
— **tarde**   later
masivo(a)   massive
matasellos (*m.*)   postmark
matemáticas (*f. pl.*)   mathematics
materia (*f.*)   subject (*in school*)
— **prima** (*f.*)   raw material
material (*m.*)   material
matrícula (*f.*)   registration; registration fees; tuition
matricularse   to register (*for school*)
matrimonio (*m.*)   married couple
máximo(a)   maximum
mayo   May
mayonesa (*f.*)   mayonnaise
mayor   older
la — parte   the majority; most
— **de edad**   of age
mayoría (*f.*)   majority
mayorista (*m., f.*)   wholesaler
mecánico(a) (*m., f.*)   mechanic

mecanógrafo(a) (*m., f.*)   typist
media (*f.*)   stocking
mediano(a)   medium, average
medianoche (*f.*)   midnight
mediante   through
medicamento (*m.*)   medicine, drug
medicina (*f.*)   medicine; drug
médico(a)   medical; (*m., f.*) medical doctor
medida (*f.*)   measure; measurement; dimension;
  size
medio(a)   half
  media hora   half an hour
  medio tiempo   part-time
mediodía (*m.*)   noon
medios (*m. pl.*)   means; system
  — de transporte (*m. pl.*)   means of
    transportation
  — publicitarios (*m. pl.*)   advertising media
medir (e:i)   to measure
mejor   better, best
mejorar   to improve
  —se   to get better, to improve (*health*)
melocotón (*m.*)   peach
melón de agua (*m.*)   watermelon
membrete (*m.*)   letterhead
memorando (*m.*)   memorandum
memoria (*f.*)   memory
mencionar   to mention
menor   less; younger
  — de edad (*m., f.*)   minor
menos (de)   least; less (than)
mensaje (*m.*)   message
mensual (*adj.*)   monthly
mensualmente (*adv.*)   monthly

menú (*m.*)   menu
menudeo (*m.*)   retail
menudo (*m.*)   small change (*Cuba*)
mercadería (*f.*)   merchandise
mercado (*m.*)   market
mercancía (*f.*)   merchandise; (*pl.*) goods
mermelada (*f.*)   marmalade
mero (*m.*)   grouper
mes (*m.*)   month
  al —   monthly
mesa (*f.*)   table
  — de centro (*f.*)   coffee table
  — de noche (*f.*)   night table, night stand
mesero(a) (*m., f.*)   waiter (waitress)
mesita (*f.*)   lap table
  — de noche (*f.*)   night table, night stand
metro (*m.*)   meter
mexicano(a)   Mexican
México   Mexico
mi(s)   my
microonda (*f.*)   microwave
miembro (*m.*)   member
mientras   while
  — tanto   in the meantime
mil   one thousand
milagro (*m.*)   miracle
milanesa (*f.*)   breaded veal cutlet
milla (*f.*)   mile
millaje (*m.*)   mileage
mineral (*m.*)   mineral
mínimo (*m.*)   minimum
minorista (*m.*)   retailer
minuto (*m.*)   minute
mirar(se)   to look at (oneself)

miscelánea (*f.*)   miscellany
mismo(a)   same
  él (ella) —   himself (herself)
mitad (*f.*)   half
mixto(a)   mixed
mochila (*f.*)   backpack, knapsack
modelo (*m.*)   model
módem (*m.*)   modem
modernizar   modernize
moderno(a)   modern
modista (*m., f.*)   dressmaker
mojado(a)   wet
moler (o:ue)   to grind
molestar(se)   to bother
momento (*m.*)   moment
  un —   one moment, just a moment
moneda (*f.*)   currency; coin
  — fraccionaria (*f.*)   small change
monitor (*m.*)   monitor
montaña (*f.*)   mountain
montar a caballo   to ride a horse
montar en bicicleta   to ride a bicycle
monumento (*m.*)   monument
morado(a)   purple
mordida (*f.*)   bribe (*Méx.*)
moreno(a)   dark-skinned, olive-skinned
morir(se) (o:ue)   to die
  — de hambre   to starve
mostaza (*f.*)   mustard
mostrador (*m.*)   counter
mostrar (o:ue)   to show
motín (*m.*)   riot
motivo (*m.*)   reason
moto (motocicleta) (*f.*)   motorcycle

motor (*m.*)   motor, engine
　　— de arranque (*m.*)   starter
mozo(a) (*m., f.*)   waiter (waitress)
muchacho(a) (*m., f.*)   boy, girl; young man, young
　　woman
mucho(a)   much, a lot
　　Mucho gusto en conocerle.   Pleased to meet
　　you.
muchos(as)   many
　　muchas gracias   thank you very much
mudarse   to move (*i.e., from one house to another*)
mueblería (*f.*)   furniture factory or store
muebles (*m. pl.*)   furniture
muerte (*f.*)   death
muerto(a)   dead
muestra (*f.*)   sample
mujer (*f.*)   woman
muletas (*f. pl.*)   crutches
multa (*f.*)   (traffic) fine, ticket; penalty
mundial   worldwide
mundo (*m.*)   world
　　— de las empresas (*m.*)   corporate world
　　todo el —   the world over
municipal   municipal
muñeca (*f.*)   wrist
museo (*m.*)   museum
musical   musical
músico(a) (*m.,f.*)   musician
muy   very
　　— bien   very well

N

nacer   to be born

nacimiento (*m.*)   birth
nacional   national
nacionalidad (*f.*)   nationality
nada   nothing
  — **más**   nothing else
nadar   to swim
nadie   nobody, no one
naranja (*f.*)   orange
nariz (*f.*)   nose
natación (*f.*)   swimming
nativo(a)   native
náusea (*f.*)   nausea
navajita (*f.*)   razor blade
Navidad (*f.*)   Christmas
necesario(a)   necessary, needed
necesidad (*f.*)   necessity, need
necesitar   to need
negar (e:ie)   to deny
negociar   to negotiate
negocio (*m.*)   business
negro(a)   black
nervioso(a)   nervous
neumático (*m.*)   tire
nevada (*f.*)   snow storm
ni   neither, nor
  — **... tampoco**   not either, neither
ningún, ninguno(a)   none
niño(a) (*m., f.*)   boy, girl; child
nivel (*m.*)   level
no   no, not
  — **fumar**   no smoking
  — **funciona.**   It's out of order., It doesn't
    work.
  — **hay apuro (prisa).**   There's no hurry.

— **importa.** It doesn't matter.
— **obstante** nevertheless
— **sirve.** It's no good., It's useless.
nocaut (*m.*) knockout (*boxing*)
noche (*f.*) night
nombrar to name, to appoint; to retain (*a lawyer*)
nombre (*m.*) name; noun
nómina (*f.*) payroll
noreste (*m.*) northeast
normal normal
noroeste (*m.*) northwest
norte (*m.*) north
norteamericano(a) (North) American
nos to us
nota (*f.*) grade
notablemente notably
noticia(s) (*f.*) news
— **policiales** (*f. pl.*) police news
novela (*f.*) novel
noventa ninety
noviembre November
novio(a) (*m., f.*) fiancé(e); boyfriend, girlfriend
nublado cloudy
nuestro(a) our
nueve nine
nuevo(a) new
nuevo peso (*m.*) currency of Mexico
nuevo sol (*m.*) currency of Peru
nuez (*f.*) nut
número (*m.*) number
— **de teléfono** (*m.*) telephone number
nunca never

O

o or, either

objeto (*m.*) object

obsoleto(a) obsolete

obtener to obtain, to get

ochenta eighty

ocho eight

octubre October

ocupación (*f.*) occupation

ocupado(a) busy

ocurrir to occur, to happen

oeste (*m.*) west

oferta (*f.*) offer, bid; deal

oficial (*m., f.*) officer

   — de guardia (*m., f.*) officer on duty

   — del banco (*m., f.*) bank officer

oficina (*f.*) office

   — de cambio (*f.*) money exchange office

   — de correos (*f.*) post office

   — de turismo (*f.*) tourist office

   — principal (*f.*) main office (*Puerto Rico*)

oficinista (*m., f.*) office clerk

ofrecer to have available

oído (*m.*) (inner) ear; hearing

Ojalá I hope; if only

   — que sí. I hope so.

ojo (*m.*) eye

olla (*f.*) pot

olvidar(se) (de) to forget

ómnibus (*m.*) bus

once eleven

opción (*f.*) option

operación (*f.*) operation

operador(a) (*m., f.*) operator
operar to operate
optimista (*m., f.*) optimist
orden (*f.*) order
   — de compra (*f.*) purchase order
ordenador (*m.*) computer (*España*)
   — portátil (*m.*) laptop computer
ordenar to order
oreja (*f.*) ear
organizar to organize
órgano (*m.*) organ
orgullo (*m.*) pride
origen (*m.*) origin
oro (*m.*) gold
orquesta (*f.*) orchestra
ostra (*f.*) oyster
otro(a) other, another
   otra vez again
¡Oye! Listen!

P

paciencia (*f.*) patience
padre (*m.*) father; (*m. pl.*) parents
pagar to pay
   — a plazos to pay in installments
   — al contado to pay in cash
   — por adelantado to pay in advance
pagaré (*m.*) promissory note, I.O.U
página de la Web (*f.*) Web page
páginas amarillas (*f. pl.*) Yellow Pages
país (*m.*) country
   — que lo expide (*m.*) issuer
paisaje (*m.*) landscape

palabra (*f.*)   word
pan (*m.*)   bread
  — **francés** (*m.*)   French toast (*Méx.*)
  — **rallado** (*m.*)   bread crumbs
  — **tostado** (*m.*)   toast
panadería (*f.*)   bakery
pantalla (*f.*)   screen
pantalones (*m. pl.*)   pants, trousers
pantimedia(s) (*f.*)   pantyhose
pañuelo (*m.*)   handkerchief
papa (*f.*)   potato
  — **al horno** (*f.*)   baked potato
papá (*m.*)   dad, father
papas fritas (*f. pl.*)   French fries
papel (*m.*)   paper
  — **de carta** (*m.*)   writing paper
  — **higiénico** (*m.*)   toilet paper
paquete (*m.*)   package
par (*m.*)   pair
para   in order to, for, to
  — **acá**   toward here, on the way here
  — **conversar**   to talk
  — **que**   so that, in order to
  ¿— **qué?**   what for?
  — **uso personal**   for personal use
parabrisas (*m. sing.*)   windshield
parachoques (*m. sing.*)   bumper
parada (*f.*)   (bus) stop
  — **de taxis** (*f.*)   taxi stop
parar   to stop
parecer   to seem, to appear, to look like
parentesco (*m.*)   (family) relationship
pargo (*m.*)   red snapper

pariente (*m., f.*)   relative

— **más cercano(a)** (*m., f.*)   closest relative

parque (*m.*)   park

parquímetro (*m.*)   parking meter

parte (*f.*)   part

participación (*f.*)   participation

participar   to participate

—**se**   to give notice

partido (*m.*)   game, match

pasado mañana   the day after tomorrow

pasado(a)   last, past

— **por agua**   soft-boiled

pasaje (*m.*)   ticket

— **de ida** (*m.*)   one-way ticket

— **de ida y vuelta** (*m.*)   round-trip ticket

pasajero(a) (*m., f.*)   passenger

pasaporte (*m.*)   passport

pasar   to come in; to pass; to happen

— **al mayor**   to enter in the ledger

— **el tiempo**   to pass the time

— **la aspiradora**   to vacuum

— **por**   to go through, to go by

— **una película**   to show a film

pase (*m.*)   entry; pass

— **al mayor** (*m.*)   general ledger entry

— **de abordar** (*m.*)   boarding pass

pasillo (*m.*)   hall, hallway; aisle

pasivo (*m.*)   liabilities

paso (*m.*)   step

un — **más**   one step further

pasta dentífrica (*f.*)   toothpaste

pastel (*m.*)   pie

pastilla (*f.*)   pill; microchip

patata (*f.*)   potato

patente (*f.*)   patent
patinar   to skate
patio (*m.*)   patio
pato (*m.*)   duck
patrón(ona) (*m., f.*)   employer
pavimento (*m.*)   pavement
pavo (*m.*)   turkey
peatón(ona) (*m., f.*)   pedestrian
pecho (*m.*)   chest
pedazo (*m.*)   piece
pedido (*m.*)   order; purchase order
pedir (e:i)   to ask for, to request, to order
  — **turno**   to make an appointment
pegar   to hit
peinar(se)   to comb (one's hair)
peine (*m.*)   comb
pelar   to peel
pelea (*f.*)   fight
película (*f.*)   film, movie
  — **en blanco y negro** (*f.*)   black-and-white
    film, movie
  — **en colores** (*f.*)   color film, movie
peligro (*f.*)   danger
peligroso(a)   dangerous
pelirrojo(a)   redheaded
pelo (*f.*)   hair
peluquería (*f.*)   beauty parlor; salon
peluquero(a) (*m., f.*)   hairdresser
penetrar   to penetrate, to enter (*i.e., a market*)
penicilina (*f.*)   penicillin
pensar (en) (e:ie)   to think (about); to plan, to
  intend (+ *inf.*)
pensión (*f.*)   pension; boarding house
  — **alimenticia** (*f.*)   alimony

pepino (*m.*) cucumber
pequeño(a) small, little
pera (*f.*) pear
perder (e:ie) to lose
   — el conocimiento to lose consciousness
pérdida (*f.*) loss
perdido(a) lost
  un caso perdido a lost cause
Perdón. Excuse me., Pardon me.
perdonar to forgive
perfumería (*f.*) perfume and toiletry shop
periférico (*m.*) peripheral (device)
periódicamente periodically
periódico (*m.*) newspaper
perito(a) (*m., f.*) expert witness
permanente (*f.*) permanent wave
permiso (*m.*) permit
pero but
perro(a) (*m., f.*) dog
persona (*f.*) person
personal personal; (*m.*) personnel
personalizado(a) personalized
pesa (*f.*) weight
pesar(se) to weigh (oneself)
pescadería (*f.*) fish market
pescado (*m.*) fish
pescar to fish
peseta (*f.*) currency of Spain
peso (*m.*) weight; currency of several Latin
  American countries
   — bruto (*m.*) gross weight
   — ligero (*m.*) lightweight (*boxer*)
   — muerto (*m.*) dead weight
   — neto (*m.*) net weight

petróleo (*m.*)   oil
picadillo (*m*)   ground meat
picnic (*m.*)   picnic
pie (*m.*)   foot
piedra (*f.*)   stone
pierna (*f.*)   leg
pieza   (*f.*)   part
   — de repuesto (*f.*)   spare part
pijama (*m.*)   pajama
piloto (*m., f.*)   pilot
pimienta (*f.*)   pepper
pinchado(a)   flat (*tire*)
pintado(a)   painted
pintar   to paint
pintor(a) (*m., f.*)   painter
pintura (*f.*)   paint; painting
piña (*f.*)   pineapple
piscina (*f.*)   swimming pool
piso (*m.*)   floor, story; apartment (*España*)
pito (*m.*)   horn, klaxon
pizarra (*f.*)   bulletin board, chalkboard
placa (*f.*)   license plate
plan (*m.*)   plan
plancha (*f.*)   iron
planear   to plan
planilla (*f.*)   form
   — de contribución sobre ingresos (*f.*)   tax
     return (*Puerto Rico*)
planta (*f.*)   plant; floor
   — alta (*f.*)   upstairs
   — baja (*f.*)   ground floor, downstairs
plástico (*m.*)   plastic
plata (*f.*)   silver
plátano (*m.*)   plantain, banana

platicar   to talk, to chat
platillo (*m.*)   saucer
plato (*m.*)   dish, plate
playa (*f.*)   beach
plaza (*f.*)   plaza, town or village square
plazo (*m.*)   term
pleito (*m.*)   lawsuit
pluma (*f.*)   pen
pobrecito(a) (*m., f.*)   poor thing
poco(a)   little (quantity)
  un poco   a little
pocos(as)   few
poder (o:ue)   to be able (to)
poderoso(a)   powerful
policía (*f.*)   police department; (*m., f.*) police officer
  — de tránsito (tráfico) (*m., f.*) traffic officer
póliza (*f.*)   policy
pollo (*m.*)   chicken
polvo (*m.*)   powder
poner   to put; to put on; to place
  — a la venta   to put up for sale
  — la mesa   to set the table
  — un negocio   to set up a business
  — una demanda   to file a lawsuit, to sue
  — una multa   to give a ticket
  —se a dieta   to go on a diet
  —se una inyección   to give (yourself) a shot
popular   popular
por   by; for; on; per; at (*with time*)
  — adelantado   in advance
  — aquí   around here; this way
  — ciento   percent
  — cierto   by the way

— **concepto (de)** referring to (*a specific item*), regarding
— **cualquier motivo** for any reason
— **cuestiones de negocios** for business reasons
— **eso** that's why, therefore
— **detrás** from behind
— **día** a (per) day
— **favor** please
— **fin** at last, finally
— **fuera** the outside
— **la mañana** in the morning
— **lo menos** at least
— **noche** a (per) night
— **otra parte** in addition
— **si acaso** just in case
— **suerte** luckily
— **último** finally, lastly
— **unidad** per unit
— **vía aérea (férrea, marítima)** by air (rail, boat)

¿por qué? why?
porque because
portaguantes (*m.*) glove compartment
portátil portable
porte (*m.*) postage
— **debido** postage due
— **pagado** postage paid
posdata (*f.*) postscript
posesión (*f.*) possession
posible possible
posición (*f.*) job, post, position
positivo(a) positive
postre (*m.*) dessert

postulante (*m., f.*)   applicant
practicar   to practice
   — un deporte   to play a sport
precedido(a)   preceded
precio (*m.*)   price
   — de compra (*m.*)   purchase price
   — de venta (*m.*)   selling price
precisamente   precisely, exactly
preferible   preferable
preferir (e:ie)   to prefer
pregunta (*f.*)   question
preguntar   to ask (*a question*)
   —se   to wonder, to ask oneself
premeditado(a)   premeditated
premio (*m.*)   prize
prenda de vestir (*f.*)   garment, clothing
prender fuego a   to set fire to
prender la luz   to turn on the light
preocupado(a)   worried
preocuparse   to worry
preparar(se)   to get ready, to prepare
presentación (*f.*)   presentation; appearance
presentar   to present
presidente (*m., f.*)   president
presilla (*f.*)   staple (*Cuba*)
presilladora (*f.*)   stapler (*Cuba*)
presión (*f.*)   (blood) pressure
prestamista (*m., f.*)   lender; pawn broker
préstamo (*m.*)   loan
prestar   to lend
   — atención   to pay attention
presupuesto (*m.*)   estimate; budget
prima (*f.*)   premium
primer(o)(a)   first

primer día de clases (*m.*)   first day of classes
primer piso (*m.*)   first floor
primera clase (*f.*)   first class
primero (*adv.*)   first
primo(a) (*m., f.*)   cousin
principalmente   principally, mostly
prisa (*f.*)   haste
privado(a)   private
probabilidad de vida (*f.*)   life expectancy
probador (*m.*)   fitting room
probar(se) (o:ue)   to try; to try on
problema (*m.*)   problem
procedencia (*f.*)   origin
procesamiento de textos (*m.*)   word processing
producto (*m.*)   product
profesional (*m., f.*)   professional
profesionalista (*m., f.*)   professional
profesor(a) (*m., f.*)   professor
prognóstico (*m.*)   forecast
programa (*m.*)   program; software
  **— de manejo (administración) de base de
    datos** (*m.*)   database management program
programador(a) (*m., f.*)   programmer
prohibido(a)   prohibited, forbidden
prolongar   to prolong
promedio (*m.*)   grade point average
pronto   soon
propaganda (*f.*)   advertisement; advertising;
    publicity
propiedad (*f.*)   property
propietario(a) (*m., f.*)   owner
propina (*f.*)   tip
propósito (*m.*)   intention
próspero(a)   prosperous

proteína (*f.*)   protein
proveedor(a) (*m., f.*)   supplier; provider
proximidad (*f.*)   proximity
próximo(a)   next
prueba (*f.*)   proof; test
publicar   to publish
publicidad (*f.*)   advertising; publicity
público(a)   public
pueblo (*m.*)   town
puente (*m.*)   bridge
puerco (*m.*)   pork
puerta (*f.*)   door; gate (*at an airport*)
    — de salida (*f.*)   boarding gate
pues   because; since; well . . .
puesto (*m.*)   post; job, position
    — de revistas (*m.*)   magazine stand
    — desempeñado (*m.*)   position held
pulgada (*f.*)   inch
pulsera (*f.*)   bracelet
puré de papas (*m.*)   mashed potatoes

Q

que   than; that; which
    — pasa   passing by
    — viene   next
qué   what; which; how
    ¡**— bueno!**   That's good!
    ¡**— casualidad!**   What a coincidence!
    ¿**— hay de nuevo?**   What's new?
    ¿**— hora es?**   What time is it?
    ¡**— lástima!**   What a pity!
    ¡**— lío!**   What a mess!

¿**— número calza?** What size shoe do you wear?

¿**— se le ofrece?** What can I do for you?

¿**— será de... ?** What will become of . ?

¿**— tal?** How's it going?, How are you doing?

quebrar (e:ie) to go bankrupt

quedar to be located; to fit

—**le chico (a uno)** to be too small

—**le grande (a uno)** to be too big

—**se** to stay, to remain

— **se con** to take, to keep

— **se en casa** to stay home

quejarse to complain

quemadura (*f.*) burn

quemar to burn

querer (e:ie) to want; to wish; to love

querido(a) dear

queso (*m.*) cheese

quetzal (*m.*) currency of Guatemala

quiebra (*f.*) bankruptcy, insolvency

¿**quién?** who?, whom?

química (*f.*) chemistry

quincenal (*adj.*) biweekly; every two weeks

quinientos(as) five hundred

quiosco (*m.*) kiosk; magazine stand

quitar(se) to take away, to take off, to remove

quizás perhaps, maybe

R

radiador (*m.*) radiator

radio (*f.*) radio

— **de batería (de pilas)** battery-operated radio

radiografía (*f.*)   X-ray
rápido (*adv.*)   fast; (*m.*) express (train)
ratón (*m.*)   mouse
raza (*f.*)   race
razón social (*f.*)   trade name
razonable   reasonable
rebajado(a)   reduced
rebajar   to reduce, to diminish
recalentarse (e:ie)   to overheat
recámara (*f.*)   room (*Méx.*)
recargo adicional (*m.*)   additional charge
recepción (*f.*)   reception desk; front desk
recepcionista (*m., f.*)   receptionist
recetar   to prescribe
recibir   to receive
recibo (*m.*)   receipt
recién   recently, newly
recientemente   recently
reclamación (*f.*)   claim
reclinar   to recline
recogedor (*m.*)   dustpan
recoger   to pick up
recomendar (e:ie)   to recommend
recordar (o:ue)   to remember
red (*f.*)   Internet
reembolso (*m.*)   refund; reimbursement
referencia (*f.*)   reference
   con — a   in regard to
refresco (*m.*)   soda, soft drink
refrigerador (*m.*)   refrigerator
regalar   to give (*a gift*)
regalo (*m.*)   gift
registrar   to register; to file
registro (*m.*)   register

regresar   to return, to come (go) back
regulación (*f.*)   regulation
rehusar   to refuse
relación (*f.*)   relation
relacionado   related
rellenar   to fill out (*a form*)
relleno(a)   stuffed
reloj (*m.*)   watch, clock
   — de pulsera (*m.*)   wristwatch
remitente (*m., f.*)   sender
remodelar   to remodel
remolacha (*f.*)   beet
remolcador (*m.*)   tow truck
remolcar   to tow
rendimiento (*m.*)   yield
rendir (e:i) informe   to report, to give an
   account
renglón (*m.*)   line (*of merchandise*); item
renta (*f.*)   revenue; income
   — vitalicia (*f.*)   life annuity
rentar   to rent
renunciar (a)   to resign (from)
reo(a) (*m., f.*)   defendant (*in a criminal case*)
reorganizar   to reorganize
reparación (*f.*)   repair
   taller de — (*m.*)   repair shop
reparar   to repair
repartir   to divide
réplica (*f.*)   replica, reproduction
repollo (*m.*)   cabbage
reportar   to report
representar   to represent
República Dominicana (*f.*)   Dominican
   Republic

repuesto (*m.*)   spare part
requerir (e:ie)   to require
requisito (*m.*)   requirement
res (*m.*)   beef
rescate (*m.*)   surrender value
reserva (*f.*)   reservation
reservación (*f.*)   reservation
reservar   to reserve
residencia universitaria (*f.*)   dormitory
residencial   residential
resolver (o:ue)   to solve
respirar   to breathe
 — **hondo**   to take a deep breath
responsabilidad (*f.*)   responsibility
 — **civil** (*f.*)   liability
reponsabilizarse   to take responsibility for
responsable   responsible
respuesta (*f.*)   answer
restaurante (*m.*)   restaurant
restitución (*f.*)   restitution
restorán (*m.*)   restaurant
resultar   to follow, to result
resumen (*m.*)   resumé
retiro (*m.*)   retirement; withdrawal
reunión (*f.*)   meeting
revelar   to develop (*film*)
revisar   to check
revista (*f.*)   magazine
revuelto(a)   scrambled
rico(a)   tasty, delicious
ridículo(a)   ridiculous
riego automático (*m.*)   automatic sprinkler
riesgo (*m.*)   risk
río (*m.*)   river

robar   to steal, to rob
robo (*m.*)   theft, burglary, robbery
rodilla (*f.*)   knee
rojo(a)   red
rollo de película (*m*)   roll of film
romper(se)   to break
ron (*m.*)   rum
ropa (*f.*)   clothes, clothing
   — interior (*f.*)   underwear
   — para damas (*f.*)   ladies' clothing
rosado(a)   pink
roto(a)   broken, torn
rotura (*f.*)   breakage
rubio(a)   blond(e)
rudimentario(a)   rudimentary
ruido (*m.*)   noise
ruta (*f.*)   route

S

sábado (*m.*)   Saturday
sábana (*f.*)   sheet
saber   to know (*a fact*)
sabroso(a)   tasty, delicious
sacar   to take out
   — el dinero   to withdraw money
   — la basura   to take out the trash
   — la cuenta   to add up
   — la lengua   to stick out one's tongue
   — pasaje   to buy (get) a ticket
   — seguro   to take out insurance
   — una nota   to get a grade
sacrificar(se)   to sacrifice (oneself)
sacudir los muebles   to dust the furniture

sal (*f.*)   salt
sala (*f.*)   room; living room
  — **de emergencia** (*f.*)   emergency room
  — **de estar** (*f.*)   family room
salario (*m.*)   salary
salchicha (*f.*)   sausage
saldo (*m.*)   balance
salida (*f.*)   departure; exit
salir   to go out, to leave
salmón (*m.*)   salmon
salón (*m.*)   salon
  — **de belleza** (*m.*)   beauty parlor; salon
  — **de estar** (*m.*)   family room
  — **de exhibición** (*m.*)   showroom, exhibition
    hall
salsa (*f.*)   sauce
  — **de tomate** (*f.*)   tomato sauce
salud (*f.*)   health; (*as a toast*) Cheers!
saludar   to greet; to say hello
saludo (*m.*)   greeting; salutation
salvavidas (*m.*)   life preserver
sandalia (*f.*)   sandal
sandía (*f.*)   watermelon
sándwich (*m.*)   sandwich
sangrar   to bleed
sartén (*f.*)   frying pan
sastre (*m.*)   tailor
satisfecho(a)   satisfied
se alquila   for rent
se vende   for sale
secador (*m.*)   (hair) dryer
secadora (*f.*)   (clothes) dryer
sección (*f.*)   section
  — **de (no) fumar** (*f.*)   (no) smoking section

seco(a) dry
secretario(a) (*m., f.*) secretary
sed (*f.*) thirst
seguir (e:i) to follow, to continue
— **derecho** to continue (to go) straight
ahead
según as; according to; depending on
— **se reciben** as they are received (come in)
segundo(a) second
seguro (*m.*) insurance
— **colectivo** (*m.*) group insurance
— **de accidentes de trabajo** (*m.*) workers'
compensation insurance
— **de grupo** (*m.*) group insurance
— **de salud** (*m.*) health insurance
— **de vida** (*m.*) life insurance
— **dotal** (*m.*) endowment insurance
— **médico** (*m.*) medical insurance
— **Social** (*m.*) Social Security
seguro(a) safe; sure, certain
seis six
seiscientos(as) six hundred
seleccionar to select
sello (*m.*) (postage) stamp
semáforo (*m.*) traffic light
semana (*f.*) week
semanal (*adj.*) weekly
semestre (*m.*) semester
sentar(se) (e:ie) to seat, to sit (down)
sentir(se) (e:ie) to feel; to regret
señal (*f.*) sign, signal
— **de parada** (*f.*) stop sign
— **de tráfico** (*f.*) traffic sign
señor (Sr.) (*m.*) Mr., sir, gentleman

señora (Sra.) (*f.*)   Mrs., madam, lady, ma'am
señorita (Srta.) (*f.*)   Miss, young lady
separado(a)   separate
septiembre   September
ser   to be
   — **la(s) (+ *time*)**   to be (+ *time*)
   — **una lástima**   to be a pity
serio(a)   serious
servicio (*m.*)   service; bathroom (toilet)
   — **de habitación** (*m.*)   room service
servilleta (*f.*)   napkin
servir (e:i)   to serve
   para —   at your service
   — **de...**   to be a(n) . . .
si   if, whether
   — **es posible**   if possible
sí   yes
siempre   always
siesta (*f.*)   nap
siete   seven
significar   to mean
silenciador (*m.*)   muffler
silla (*f.*)   chair
simpático(a)   nice; charming; fun to be with
sin   without
   — **remedio**   without hope
síntoma (*m.*)   symptom
Sírvase   Please
sirviente(a) (*m., f.*)   servant
sistema (*m.*)   system
   — **de suspensión** (*m.*)   suspension
   — **operativo** (*m.*)   operating system
situación (*f.*)   situation
situado(a)   situated

soborno (*m.*)   bribe
sobre   about; on; on top of; over; (*m.*) envelope
   — todo   especially, above all
sobregiro (*m.*)   overdraft
sobrepasar   to surpass
social   social
   Seguro — (*m.*)   Social Security
sociedad (*f.*)   society; company
   — anónima (S.A.) (*f.*)   corporation
   — de responsabilidad limitada (S.R.L.) (*f.*)
      limited liability company
   — regular colectiva (*f.*)   general partnership
socio(a) (*m., f.*)   member; partner
¡Socorro!   Help!
sofá (*m.*)   sofa
sofisticado(a)   sophisticated
solamente   only
soleado(a)   sunny
solicitante (*m., f.*)   applicant
   — de cuenta conjunta (*m., f.*)   co-applicant
      for joint account
solicitar   to ask for; to apply for
solicitud (*f.*)   application
solo(a)   alone
sólo   only
soltero(a)   single
sondeo de la opinión pública (*m.*)   poll; survey
sopa (*f.*)   soup
soplado(a)   blown (*glass*)
soporte (*m.*)   support
   — físico (*m.*)   hardware
   — lógico (*m.*)   software
sortija (*f.*)   ring
sospechar   to suspect

su   his; her; their; your (*form.*)
subdesarrollado(a)   underdeveloped
subir   to climb; to go up; to get on or in; to board
   (*a plane*)
   — el volumen   to turn up the volume
subterráneo (*m.*)   subway
subtotal (*m.*)   subtotal
suceder   to happen
sucio(a)   dirty
sucre (*m.*)   currency of Ecuador
sucursal (*f.*)   branch
suegro(a) (*m., f.*)   father-in-law, mother-in-law
sueldo (*m.*)   salary
   — mensual (*m.*)   monthly salary
suelo (*m.*)   ground, floor
suelto (*m.*)   small change (*Puerto Rico*)
suéter (*m.*)   sweater
suficiente   enough, sufficient
sufrimiento (*m.*)   suffering
sufrir   to suffer
sugerente   catchy; suggestive
sugerir (e:ie)   to suggest
sugestivo(a)   catchy; suggestive
suicidio (*m.*)   suicide
sujetapapeles (*m.*)   paper clip
suma (*f.*)   amount
suministrador(a) (*m., f.*)   provider, supplier
superar   to exceed
supermercado (*m.*)   supermarket
supersticioso(a)   superstitious
suponer   to suppose
sur (*m.*)   south
sureste (*m.*)   southeast
suroeste (*m.*)   southwest

suyo(a)   his; hers; one's; yours (*form.*)

T

tabla de cotizaciones (*f.*)   currency exchange table

tablilla de avisos (*f.*)   bulletin board

tachuela (*f.*)   thumbtack (*Puerto Rico*)

talla (*f.*)   size

taller de reparaciones (*m.*)   auto shop; mechanic's shop

talonario de cheques (*m.*)   checkbook

tamaño (*m.*)   size

también   also; too

tampoco   neither, either

tan   so; such a
  — **...como**   as . . . as
  — **pronto como**   as soon as

tanque (*m.*)   tank

tanto(a)   so much

tantos(as)   so many

tapicería (*f.*)   upholstery

tara (*f.*)   tare

tarde   late; (*f.*) afternoon

tarifa (*f.*)   fare; rate; tariff; toll

tarjeta (*f.*)   card
  — **de crédito** (*f.*)   credit card
  — **de embarque** (*f.*)   boarding pass
  — **de registro (huésped)** (*f.*)   registration card
  — **de residente** (*f.*)   resident card
  — **postal** (*f.*)   postcard
  — **verde** (*f.*)   green card

tasa (*f.*) rate
   — de cambios (*f.*) exchange rate
   — de interés (*f.*) interest rate
tasador(a) (*m., f.*) appraiser
tasar to value; to appraise
tatuaje (*m.*) tattoo
taxi (*m.*) taxi
taxímetro (*m.*) taximeter
taxista (*m., f.*) taxi driver
taza (*f.*) cup
té (*m.*) tea
teatro (*m.*) theater
techo (*m.*) roof
tecla (*f.*) key
teclado (*m.*) keyboard
técnico(a) (*m., f.*) technician
teja (*f.*) roof tile
tejido (*m.*) fabric
tela (*f.*) fabric
telecomunicaciones (*f. pl.*) telecommunications
telefonista (*m., f.*) telephone operator
teléfono (*m.*) telephone
telegrama (*m.*) telegram
televisión (*f.*) television
televisor (*m.*) TV set
   — portátil (*m.*) portable television set
temblor (*m.*) earthquake
temer to fear, to be afraid of
   Me temo que... I am afraid that . . .
temperatura (*f.*) temperature
temprano early
tenedor (*m.*) fork
tenedor(a) de libros (*m., f.*) bookkeeper
tener to have, to hold

— **algo que declarar**   to have something to declare
— **calor**   to be hot
— **casa propia**   to own a house
—   **de atraso**   to be (*time quantity*) behind (schedule)
— **en cuenta**   to take into account
— **frío**   to be cold
— **hambre**   to be hungry
— **la culpa**   to be at fault, to be guilty
— **lugar**   to take place
— **paciencia**   to be patient
— **prisa**   to be in a hurry
— **que (+ *inf.*)**   to have to (do something)
— **razón**   to be right
— **retraso**   to be behind schedule
— **sed**   to be thirsty
— **suerte**   to be in luck, to be lucky
tenis (*m.*)   tennis
tercer(o)(a)   third
   tercera persona   third party
tercero(a) (*m., f.*)   third party
terminar   to finish, to end
término (*m.*)   term
termita (*f.*)   termite
ternera (*f.*)   veal
terraza (*f.*)   terrace
terremoto (*m.*)   earthquake
testamento (*m.*)   will
testigo (*m., f.*)   witness
tétano (*m.*)   tetanus
tiempo (*m.*)   time
   — **extra**   overtime

tienda (*f.*)   store
— **de campaña** (*f.*)   tent
tierra (*f.*)   land
timbre (*m.*)   (postage) stamp (*Méx.*)
timón (*m.*)   steering wheel
tintorería (*f.*)   dry cleaners
típico(a)   typical, model
tipo (*m.*)   type
— **de interés** (*m.*)   interest rate
tirada (*f.*)   circulation
tirar basura   to throw (out) garbage, to litter
título (*m.*)   title
TLCAN (Tratado de Libre Comercio de América del Norte) (*m.*)   NAFTA (North American Free Trade Agreement)
toalla (*f.*)   towel
tobillo (*m.*)   ankle
tocadiscos (*m.*)   record player
tocino (*m.*)   bacon
todavía   still, yet
todo   all; everything
todos(as)   all (of them); every; everybody, everyone; all
todos los días   every day
tomar   to have something to drink; to take (*a bus, train, etc.*)
— **una decisión**   to make a decision
tomate (*m.*)   tomato
Tome asiento.   Have a seat.
tonelada (*f.*)   ton
torcer (o:ue)   to twist
tornado (*m.*)   tornado
toronja (*f.*)   grapefruit
torta (*f.*)   cake

tortilla (*f.*) tortilla (*Méx.*); omelet (*España*)
 — **a la española** (*f.*) omelet with potatoes
 — **a la francesa** (*f.*) plain omelet
tos (*f.*) cough
tostada (*f.*) piece of toast
tostadora (*f.*) toaster
total (*m.*) total
totalmente completely, totally
trabajador(a) (*m., f.*) worker
trabajar to work
 — **por cuenta propia** to be self-employed
trabajo (*m.*) work, job
tradicional traditional
traductor(a) (*m., f.*) translator
traer to bring
tráfico (*m.*) traffic
traje (*m.*) suit
trámite (*m.*) procedure
transacción (*f.*) transaction
transbordar to transfer
transbordo (*m.*) transfer
transeúnte (*m., f.*) passer-by
transferencia (*f.*) transfer
transformador (*m.*) transformer
tránsito (*m.*) transit, traffic
transmisión (*f.*) transmission (gear)
transparente transparent
transportar to transport
transporte (*m.*) transport; shipping
 — **por tierra** (*m.*) land transportation
trasbordar to change (*trains, buses, etc.*); to transfer
trasladar to move, to relocate
traspaso (*m.*) transfer

**Tratado de Libre Comercio de América del
Norte** (*m.*)   North American Free Trade
Agreement (NAFTA)

tratar   to deal

　— **de**   to try (to)

　—**se de**   to be a question of

trece   thirteen

treinta   thirty

tren (*m.*)   train, railroad

trescientos(as)   three hundred

trimestre (*m.*)   quarter (*in school*)

trozo (*m.*)   piece

trucha (*f.*)   trout

tu   your (*fam.*)

tú   you (*fam.*)

tubo de escape (*m.*)   exhaust pipe

turbulencia (*f.*)   turbulence

turista (*m., f.*)   tourist

turno (*m.*)   appointment; shift

tutor (*m.*)   guardian

U

Ud.   you (*form. sing.*)

Uds.   you (*pl.*)

último(a)   last (*in a series*)

un(o)(a)   a (an); one

únicamente   only

único(a)   only one

　hijo(a) — (*m., f.*)   only child

　lo —   only thing

unidad (*f.*)   unit; (college) credit

universidad (*f.*)   university

unos(as) some, several (*with nouns*); about (*with numbers*)

urgencia (*f.*) urgency

usado(a) used

usar to use; to wear

uso (*m.*) use

usualmente usually

utilidad (*f.*) profit

   — **bruta** (*f.*) gross profit

   — **neta** (*f.*) net profit

utilizar to use; to utilize

uvas (*f. pl.*) grapes

V

vacaciones (*f. pl.*) vacation

vacío(a) empty, vacant

vainilla (*f.*) vanilla

vajilla (*f.*) (set of) dishes

vale (*m.*) voucher

valer to be worth, to be valid

   — **la pena** to be worth it

válido(a) valid

valija (*f.*) suitcase

valioso(a) valuable

valla (*f.*) billboard

valor (*m.*) value, worth

variable variable

variar to change, to vary

variedad (*f.*) variety

varios(as) several, various

vaso (*m.*) glass

vecindario (*m.*) neighborhood

vecino(a) (*m., f.*) neighbor

vegetales (*m. pl.*)   vegetables
veinte   twenty
velices (*m. pl.*)   baggage (*Méx.*)
velocidad (*f.*)   speed
   — máxima (*f.*)   speed limit
vencer   to defeat
vencido(a)   due
vender   to sell
   se vende   for sale
venir   to come
venta (*f.*)   sale
ventaja (*f.*)   advantage
ventanilla (*f.*)   service window; window (*on a plane, etc.*)
ver   to see
   a —   let's see
verano (*m.*)   summer
verbo (*m.*)   verb
verdad (*f.*)   truth
   ¿—?   right?
verdadero(a)   true
verde   green
verdulería (*f.*)   green grocery
verdura (*f.*)   vegetable
vereda (*f.*)   sidewalk
veredicto (*m.*)   verdict
vermut (*m.*)   vermouth
versión (*f.*)   version
vestíbulo (*m.*)   lobby
vestido (*m.*)   dress
vestidura (*f.*)   upholstery
vestir(se) (**e:i**)   to dress, to get dressed
vez (*f.*)   time
vía: una —   one way (*street*)

viajante (*m., f.*)   traveling salesperson
viajar   to travel
viaje (*m.*)   travel, trip
  — de negocios (*m.*)   business trip
vibración (*f.*)   vibration
vida (*f.*)   life
videograbadora (*f.*)   VCR
vidriera (*f.*)   store window
vidrio (*m.*)   glass
viejo(a)   old
viernes (*m.*)   Friday
vino (*m.*)   wine
  — blanco (*m.*)   white wine
  — tinto (*m.*)   red wine
violación (*f.*)   rape; violation
violado(a)   raped
visa (*f.*)   visa
visitar   to visit
vista (*f.*)   view
  — a la calle (*f.*)   exterior (street) view
  — interior (*f.*)   interior view
vitamina (*f.*)   vitamin
viudo(a) (*m., f.*)   widower, widow
vivienda (*f.*)   housing
vivir   to live
vocabulario (*m.*)   vocabulary
volante (*m.*)   steering wheel
volar (o:ue)   to fly
voltear   to turn
  voltee...   turn . . .
volumen (*m.*)   volume
volver (o:ue)   to come (go) back, to return
vomitar   to vomit
voz (*f.*)   voice

vuelo (*m.*)   flight
vuelto (*m.*)   change

Y

y   and
ya   already
   ¡**— lo creo!**   I'll say!, I believe it!
   — lo sé   I know
   — no   no longer
   — voy   I'm coming
yo   I
   — solo(a)   just me
yogur (*m.*)   yogurt

Z

zacate (*m.*)   lawn; grass (*Méx.*)
zanahoria (*f.*)   carrot
zapatería (*f.*)   shoe store or factory
zapato (*m.*)   shoe
zona (*f.*)   zone
   — de estacionamiento (*f.*)   parking lot

English–Spanish

A

a   por; un, una
- **— day**   por día
- **— little**   un poco
- **— lot**   mucho(a)
- **— night (per night)**   por noche
- **— thousand**   mil
- **— while later**   al rato

about   acerca de; alrededor de; de unos(as); sobre
- **— ... (+ *number*)**   unos... (+ *number*)
- **— that (the matter)**   al respecto

above   sobre
- **— all**   sobre todo

absence   ausencia (*f.*)

absurd   absurdo(a)

accelerator   acelerador (*m.*)

accept   aceptar

acceptance   aceptación (*f.*)

access   acceso (*m.*)

accessory   accesorio (*m.*)

accident   accidente (*m.*)

accompany   acompañar

according to   según; al ritmo de

account   cuenta (*f.*)
- **— payable**   cuenta a pagar (*f.*)
- **— receivable**   cuenta a cobrar (*f.*)

accountant   contador(a) (*m., f.*)

accounting   contabilidad (*f.*); (*adj.*) contable

accredit   acreditar

ache   doler (o:ue)

acknowledgement of receipt acuse de recibo (*m.*)

act of God fenómeno natural (*m.*), fuerza mayor (*f.*)

ad anuncio (*m.*), aviso (*m.*)

adapt adaptar

add agregar

  — up sacar la cuenta

addition: in — to aparte

additional adicional

  — charge recargo adicional (*m.*)

address dirección (*f.*), domicilio (*m.*)

addressee destinatario(a) (*m., f.*)

adequate maintenance mantenimiento adecuado (*m.*)

adjective adjetivo (*m.*)

adjusted gross income ingreso ajustado bruto (*m.*)

adjustment ajuste (*m.*)

administrator administrador(a) (*m., f.*)

admit admitir

advance payment anticipo (*m.*)

advantage ventaja (*f.*)

advertise anunciar

advertisement propaganda (*f.*)

advertising publicidad (*f.*), propaganda (*f.*)

  — agency agencia de publicidad (f.)

  — media medio publicitario (*m.*)

advice consejo (*m.*), asesoramiento (*m.*)

advise aconsejar

adviser consejero(a) (*m., f.*)

aerobic dance danza aeróbica (*f.*)

affect afectar

affectionately cariñosamente

after después de
afternoon tarde (*f.*)
afterwards después
again de nuevo, otra vez
against contra
age edad (*f.*)
agency agencia (*f.*)
agent agente (*m., f.*)
agree (on) convenir (en), estar de acuerdo
air (*adj.*) aéreo(a); aire (*m.*)
   — conditioning aire acondicionado (*m.*)
   — mail correo aéreo (*m.*)
airline línea aérea (*f.*), aerolínea (*f.*)
airport aeropuerto (*m.*)
airsick mareado(a)
airsickness mareo (*m.*)
aisle pasillo (*m.*)
   — seat asiento de pasillo (*m.*)
alcohol alcohol (*m.*)
alcoholic alcohólico(a)
alimony pensión alimenticia (*f.*)
all todos(as); todo (*m.*)
   — of them todos(as)
allergic alérgico(a)
allow dejar
almost casi
   — raw casi crudo(a)
alone solo(a)
already ya
also también
although aunque
altitude altura (*f.*)
always siempre
ambulance ambulancia (*f.*)

American americano(a)
among entre
amount importe (*m.*), suma (*f.*)
amusing divertido(a)
and y
anesthesia anestesia (*f.*)
angry enfadado(a), enojado(a)
animal animal (*m.*)
ankle tobillo (*m.*)
anniversary aniversario (*m.*)
announce anunciar
another otro(a)
answer respuesta (*f.*)
answering machine máquina contestadora (*f.*)
antibiotic antibiótico (*m.*)
any algún(o)(a), cualquier(a)
  — **style** al gusto
anything cualquier cosa; algo
  — **else?** ¿Algo más?
  — **to declare?** ¿Algo que declarar?
anyway de todos modos
apartment apartamento (*m.*), piso (*m.*) (*España*)
  — **building** edificio de apartamentos (*m.*)
appear parecer; aparecer
appearance presentación (*f.*); apariencia (*f.*)
appetizer entremés (*m.*)
apple manzana (*f.*)
appliance electrodoméstico (*m.*)
applicant candidato(a) (*m.*, *f.*), aspirante (*m.*, *f.*)
application solicitud (*f.*)
apply for solicitar
appoint nombrar
appointment turno (*m.*), cita (*f.*)
appraise tasar

appraiser   tasador(a) (*m., f.*)
appropriate: if —   si procede
approval   aprobación (*f.*)
approve   aprobar (o:ue)
approximately   más o menos, unos(as)
April   abril
Arab   árabe (*m., f.*)
Arabic   árabe (*m., f.*)
area   área (*f.* but **el área**)
Argentinian   argentino(a)
arm   brazo (*m.*)
armchair   butaca (*f.*)
around   más o menos
  — here   por aquí
  — the corner   a la vuelta de la esquina
arrangement   arreglo (*m.*), iguala (*f.*) (*Cuba*)
arrival   entrada (*f.*)
arrive (in)   llegar (a)
arson   incendio premeditado (*m.*)
art   arte (*f.* but **el arte**)
artcraft   artesanía (*f.*)
article   artículo (*m.*)
as   según; como
  — a child   de niño(a)
  — always   como siempre
  — ... as   tan...como
  — of   a partir de
  — of (+ *date*)   a partir del día (+ *date*)
  — soon as   tan pronto como, en cuanto
  — they are received (come in)   según se
    reciben
  — usual   como siempre
ashtray   cenicero (*m.*)

ask (for)   pedir (e:i); solicitar
   — **a question**   preguntar
   — **oneself**   preguntarse
aspirin   aspirina (*f.*)
assault   asalto (*m.*)
assess   evaluar
assets   bienes (*m. pl.*); activo (*m.*)
assist   atender (e:ie)
assistance   ayuda (*f.*)
assistant   asistente (*m., f.*)
association   asociación (*f.*)
assume   asumir
at   a; en
   — **(+ *time*)**   a la(s) (+ *time*)
   — **fault**   culpable
   — **home**   en casa
   — **last**   por fin
   — **least**   por lo menos
   — **lunch time**   a la hora del almuerzo
   — **the end**   al final
   — **what time?**   ¿A qué hora?
   — **your expense**   a su cargo
   — **your service**   a sus órdenes, para servirle
athletic   atlético(a)
   — **meet**   competencia (*f.*)
attached   adjunto(a)
attempt   atentado (*m.*)
attend   asistir
   — **to**   atender (e:ie)
attendance   asistencia (*f.*)
attention   atención (*f.*)
August   agosto
authorize   autorizar
auto   automóvil (*m.*)

— **club**   club automovilístico (*m.*)
— **race**   carrera de automóviles (*f.*)
— **shop**   taller de mecánica (*m.*)
automate   automatizar
automatic   automático(a)
automatically   automáticamente
available   disponible; instalado(a); libre
  to have —   contar (o:ue) con
avenue   avenida (*f.*)
average   mediano(a)
avocado   aguacate (*m.*)
avoid   evitar
awarded   adjudicado(a)

B

back   espalda (*f.*)
backpack   mochila (*f.*)
bacon   tocino (*m.*)
bad   malo(a)
bad-looking   feo(a)
bag   bolsa (*f.*)
baggage   equipaje (*m.*); velices (*m. pl.*) (*Méx.*)
baked   al horno
  — **potato**   papa al horno (*f.*)
bakery   panadería (*f.*)
balance   saldo (*m.*); balance (*m.*)
  — **sheet**   balance general (*m.*)
balanced   balanceado(a)
ball bearings   caja de bolas (*f.*)
ballpoint pen   bolígrafo (*m.*)
banana   plátano (*m.*)
bank (*adj.*)   bancario(a); banco (*m.*)
  — **note**   billete (de banco) (*m.*)

— **officer** oficial de banco (*m., f.*)

banker banquero(a) (*m., f.*)

bankruptcy quiebra (*f.*), insolvencia (*f.*)

barber barbero(a)

— **shop** barbería (*f.*)

bargain ganga (*f.*)

basketball basquetbol (*m.*)

bathe bañar(se)

bathroom baño (*m.*), cuarto de baño (*m.*), servicio (*m.*), excusado (*m.*) (*Méx.*)

— **sink** lavabo (*m.*)

bathtub bañadera (*f.*)

battery acumulador (*m.*); batería (*f.*)

— **-operated radio** radio de batería (pilas) (*f.*)

bazaar bazar (*m.*)

be ser; estar; servir (e:i) de

— **a demand for** tener aceptación

— **a question of** tratarse de

— **able** poder (o:ue)

— **acquainted** conocer

— **advisable** convenir (e:ie)

— **afraid of** temer

— **afraid that . . .** temerse que...

— **at fault** tener la culpa

— **at your disposal** estar a su disposición

— (*time quantity*) **behind** (**schedule**) tener... de atraso, tener retraso

— **born** nacer

— **certain of** estar seguro(a) de

— **cold** tener frío

— **enough** alcanzar

— **glad** alegrarse

— **going** (**to do something**) ir a (+ *inf.*)

— **good for**   convenir (e:ie)
— **guilty**   tener la culpa
— **happy**   alegrarse
— **hot**   tener calor
— **hungry**   tener hambre
— **in charge (of)**   correr con
— **in luck**   tener suerte
— **in style**   estar de moda
— **lacking**   faltar
— **late (early)**   llegar tarde (temprano)
— **located**   quedar
— **lucky**   tener suerte
— **necessary (to do something)**   hay que (+ *inf.*)
— **no longer**   dejar de ser
— **on vacation**   estar de vacaciones
— **paid by you**   ir por su cuenta
— **patient**   tener paciencia
— **pleasing (to)**   gustar
— **raised**   criarse
— **right**   tener razón
— **self-employed**   trabajar por cuenta propia
— **sorry for**   lamentar
— **sure**   estar seguro(a)
— **thirsty**   tener sed
— **to one's advantage**   convenirle a uno
— **too big**   quedarle grande (a uno)
— **too small**   quedarle chico (a uno)
— **too tight**   apretar (e:ie)
— **unconscious**   perder (e:ie) el conocimiento
— **valid**   valer
— **well received**   tener aceptación
— **willing to**   estar dispuesto(a) a

— **worth (it)** valer (la pena)

beach playa (f.)

bean frijol (m.)

beard barba (f.)

beautiful bonito(a), guapo(a), hermoso(a), lindo(a)

beauty parlor peluquería (f.), salón de belleza (m.)

because porque; pues

become llegar, convertir(se) (e:ie) en

bed cama (f.)

bedroom dormitorio (m.)

— **set** juego de cuarto (dormitorio) (m.)

beef carne de res (f.); res (m.)

beer cerveza (f.)

beet remolacha (f.)

before antes (de)

— **deciding** antes de decidir

begin comenzar (e:ie), empezar (e:ie)

behind detrás de

being that cómo

believe creer

bell pepper ají (m.)

bellhop botones (m.)

belt cinturón (m.)

beneficiary beneficiario(a) (m., f.)

bequest legado (m.)

berth litera (f.)

besides además (de)

best mejor

the — **thing** lo mejor

better mejor

between entre

bicycle bicicleta (f.)

bid oferta (*f.*)
big grande
bilingual bilingüe
bill cuenta (*f.*); billete (de banco) (*m.*)
   — of exchange letra de cambio (*f*)
billboard valla (*f.*)
birth nacimiento (*m.*)
birthday cumpleaños (*m.*)
   — party fiesta de cumpleaños (*f.*)
biweekly quincenal
black negro(a)
   — and white film película en blanco y
     negro (*f.*)
   — coffee (strong) café expreso (*m.*); café
     solo (*m.*)
   in — and white en blanco y negro
blame culpa (*f.*)
blanket cobija (*f.*), frazada (*f.*), manta (*f.*)
bleach lejía (*f.*)
bleed sangrar
block cuadra (*f.*)
   three —s from a tres cuadras de
blond(e) rubio(a)
blood pressure presión (*f.*)
blouse blusa (*f.*)
blown soplado(a)
blue azul
board (a plane) subir
boarding gate puerta de salida (*f.*)
boarding house pensión (*f.*)
boarding pass pase de abordar (*m.*); tarjeta de
   embarque (*f.*)
boat barco (*m.*); buque (*m.*)

body   cuerpo (*m.*)
  — **of a car**   carrocería (*f.*)
boil   hervir (e:ie)
boiled   hervido(a)
bonbons   bombones (*m. pl.*)
bond   bono (*m.*)
book   libro (*m.*)
bookkeeper   tenedor(a) de libros (*m., f.*)
booklet   folleto (*m.*)
boot   bota (*f.*)
border   frontera (*f.*)
boss   jefe(a) (*m., f.*)
both   ambos(as)
bother   molestar(se)
bottle   botella (*f.*)
boulevard   boulevard (*m.*)
bounced check   cheque sin fondos (*m.*)
box   caja (*f.*)
boy   muchacho (*m.*), niño (*m.*)
boyfriend   novio (*m.*)
bracelet   pulsera (*f.*)
brake   freno (*m.*)
  — **fluid**   líquido de frenos (*m.*)
branch   sucursal (*f.*)
brand   marca (*f.*)
bread   pan (*m.*)
  — **crumbs**   pan rallado (*m.*)
breaded   empanizado(a)
  — **veal cutlet**   milanesa (*f.*)
break   romper
  — **down (car)**   descomponerse
breakage   rotura (*f.*)
breakfast   desayuno (*m.*)
breathe   respirar

bribe soborno (*m.*); mordida (*f.*) (*Méx.*)
brick ladrillo (*m.*)
bridge puente (*m.*)
brief breve
bring traer
broccoli brécol (*m.*). bróculi (*m.*)
broiled asado(a)
broken (down) descompuesto(a), roto(a)
broom escoba (*f.*)
broth caldo (*m.*)
brother hermano (*m.*)
brown (*adj.*) café, marrón
brush (oneself) cepillar(se)
  — **one's teeth** cepillarse los dientes
budget presupuesto (*m.*)
building edificio (*m.*); inmueble (*m.*)
built construido(a)
bulletin board pizarra (*f.*); tablilla de avisos
  (*f.*)
bumper defensa (*f.*), parachoques (*m.*)
bundle bulto (*m.*)
burglary robo (*m.*)
burn quemadura (*f.*); quemar
bus autobús (*m.*), camión (*m.*) (*Méx.*), ómnibus
  (*m.*)
  — **stop** parada (*f.*)
business negocio(s) (*m.*), firma (*f.*);
  establecimiento comercial (*m.*)
  — **administration** administración de
    empresas (*f.*)
  — **correspondence** correspondencia
    comercial (*f.*)
  — **documents** documentos mercantiles (*m.
    pl.*)

— **letter** carta de negocios (*f.*)
— **trip** viaje de negocios (*m.*)
busy ocupado(a)
but pero
butcher shop carnicería (*f.*)
butter mantequilla (*f.*)
buy comprar
— **(get) a ticket** sacar pasaje
buyer comprador(a) (*m., f.*)
buying compra (*f.*)
by por
— **a certain date** fecha fija
— **air** por vía aérea
— **boat** por vía marítma
— **rail** por vía férrea
— **the way** por cierto
Bye. Chau.

C

cabbage repollo (*m.*)
cabinet gabinete (*m.*)
cafe café (*m.*)
— **au lait** café con leche (*m.*)
cafeteria cafetería (*f.*)
cake torta (*f.*)
calculator calculador(a) (*m., f.*)
call llamar; llamada (*f.*)
— **on the phone** llamar por teléfono
calm (down) calmar(se)
calorie caloría (*f.*)
camera cámara fotográfica (*f.*)
camp acampar

campaign: promotional — campaña de promoción (*f.*)

cancel cancelar

canceled cancelado(a)

candidate candidato(a) (*m., f.*)

candy bombones (*m. pl.*)

— **store** dulcería (*f.*)

capital capital (*m.*)

car auto (*m.*), automóvil (*m.*), carro (*m.*), coche (*m.*), máquina (*f.*) (*Cuba*)

— **related** automovilístico(a)

carbohydrate carbohidrato (*m.*)

card tarjeta (*f.*)

care cuidado

cared (for) cuidado(a)

career carrera (*f.*)

carefully cuidadosamente

carpet alfombra (*f.*)

carrot zanahoria (*f.*)

carry llevar

— **out** desempeñar

carry-on bag bolso(a) (*m., f.*); bolso de mano (*m.*); maletín de mano (*m.*)

case caso (*m.*)

cash efectivo (*m.*); centavo (*m.*); dinero en efectivo (*m.*)

— **a check** cobrar un cheque

— **book** libro de caja (*m.*)

— **register** caja registradora (*f.*)

cashier cajero(a) (*m., f.*)

—'**s check** cheque de caja (*m.*)

cat gato(a) (*m., f.*)

catchy sugestivo(a); sugerente

cathedral catedral (*f.*)

cause caso (*m.*); motivo (*m.*)
caused causado(a)
caution cuidado
celebrate celebrar
celery apio (*m.*)
cent centavo (*m.*)
center of the city centro de la ciudad (*m.*)
centimeter centímetro (*m.*)
cereal cereal (*m.*)
certain seguro(a)
certainly cómo no
certificate of deposit (C.D.) certificado de
   depósito (*m.*)
certified certificado(a)
   — letter carta certificada (*f.*)
   — Public Accountant Contador(a)
     Público(a) Titulado(a) (*m., f.*)
chain cadena (*f.*)
chair silla (*f.*)
champagne champaña (*m.*)
champion campeón(ona) (*m., f.*)
change cambiar, variar; cambio (*m.*), vuelto (*m.*)
   — one's mind cambiar de idea
   — trains, buses, etc. trasbordar
charge cargar; cobrar
charity caridad (*f.*)
charming simpático(a)
chassis chasis (*m.*)
chat charlar, platicar
chauffeur chofer (*m., f.*)
cheap barato(a)
check cheque (*m.*); chequear, revisar
   — out desocupar la habitación
   — to the bearer cheque al portador (*m.*)

checkbook   chequera (*f.*); talonario de cheques
   (*m.*)
checking account   cuenta corriente (*f.*), cuenta
   de cheques (*f.*) (*Méx.*)
Cheers!   ¡Salud!
cheese   queso (*m.*)
chemistry   química (*f.*)
chest   pecho (*m.*)
   — of drawers   cómoda (*f.*)
chicken   pollo (*m.*)
   — and rice   arroz con pollo (*m.*)
chief   jefe(a) (*m., f.*)
child   niño(a) (*m., f.*)
children   hijos (*m. pl.*), niños (*m. pl.*)
chile (bell pepper)   chile (*m.*)
Chilean   chileno(a)
chocolate   chocolate (*m.*)
choose   escoger, elegir (e:i)
chop   chuleta (*f.*)
Christmas   Navidad (*f.*)
church   iglesia (*f.*)
cigarette   cigarrillo (*m.*)
circular   circular (*f.*), carta circular (*f.*)
circulation   circulación (*f.*); tirada (*f.*)
citizen   ciudadano(a) (*m., f.*)
city   ciudad (*f.*)
claim   reclamación (*f.*)
   — check (ticket)   comprobante (*m.*)
clam   almeja (*f.*)
class   clase (*f.*)
classmate   compañero(a) de clase (*m., f.*)
clause   cláusula (*f.*)
clean   limpio(a); limpiar
cleaning   limpieza (*f.*)

clear   claro(a)
clerk   empleado(a) (*m., f.*)
client   cliente(a) (*m., f.*)
climb   escalar, subir
clock   reloj (*m.*)
close   cerrar (e:ie)
close by   cercano(a)
closing   despedida (*f.*)
   — **costs**   gastos de cierre (*m. pl.*)
   — **date**   fecha de cierre (*f.*)
clothes   ropa (*f.*)
   — **dryer**   secadora (*f.*)
clothing   prenda de vestir (*f.*); ropa (*f.*)
cloudy   nublado(a)
co-applicant for joint account   solicitante de cuenta conjunta (*m., f.*)
coat   abrigo (*m.*)
cocktail   cóctel (*m.*)
coconut   coco (*m.*)
cod   bacalao (*m.*)
code   código (*m.*); clave (*f.*)
coffee   café (*m.*)
   — **shop**   cafetería (*f.*)
   — **table**   mesa de centro (*f.*)
coin   moneda (*f.*)
cold   frío(a)
collateral   aval (*m.*)
collect   cobrar
   — **on delivery (C.O.D.)**   cobrar o devolver (C.O.D.)
collection (of debts)   cobro (*m.*)
collide   chocar
cologne   colonia (*f.*)
color   color (*m.*)

— **film**   película en colores (*f.*)

comb   peine (*m.*)

— **(one's hair)**   peinar(se)

come   venir

— **(go) back**   regresar; volver (o:ue)

— **in**   pasar

comfort   comodidad (*f.*)

comfortable   cómodo(a)

coming month   el mes que viene (*m.*)

commercial   comercial

commission   comisión (*f.*)

communication   comunicación (*f.*)

compact   compacto(a)

company   firma (*f.*), compañía (*f.*), empresa (*f.*)

compare   comparar

compatible   compatible

compensate   compensar

compensation   compensación (*f.*); indemnización (*f.*)

compete   competir (e:i)

competition   competencia (*f.*)

complain   quejarse

complete   completo(a)

completely   totalmente

compound interest   interés compuesto (*m.*)

comprehensive   comprensivo(a)

computation   computación (*f.*)

computer   computador(a) (*m., f.*); ordenador (*m.*) (*España*)

— **disk(ette)**   disco (de programación) (*m.*); disquete (*m.*)

— **hardware**   equipo de computación (*m.*)

— **science**   cibernética (*f.*), informática (*f.*)

concept   concepto (*m.*)

concert concierto (*m.*)
condition condición (*f.*)
condominium condominio (*m.*)
confections dulces (*m. pl.*)
confirm confirmar
congratulations felicidades (*f. pl.*)
connect conectar
consignee consignatario(a) (*m., f.*)
consignment note (*trucking*) guía (*f.*)
consist (of) consistir (en)
consult consultar
consultation consulta (*f.*)
consulting asesoramiento (*m.*)
consume consumir
consumer consumidor(a) (*m., f.*)
contain contener
container contenedor (*m.*)
continue continuar, seguir (e:i)
  — (to go) straight ahead seguir derecho
contract contrato (*m.*)
contribution contribución (*f.*)
convenience comodidad (*f.*)
convenient conveniente
conversation conversación (*f.*)
converse conversar
cook cocinar
cookie galleta (*f.*), galletica (*f.*); galletita (*f.*)
cooperation cooperación (*f.*)
co-owner codueño(a) (*m., f.*)
copy copia (*f.*); ejemplar (*m.*)
  — machine máquina copiadora (*f.*)
cordially cordialmente
corner esquina (*f.*)
  the — of la esquina de

upper right (left) — esquina superior derecha (izquierda) (*f.*)

corporation   sociedad anónima (S.A.) (*f.*)

correspondence   correspondencia (*f.*)

cost   costo (*m.*), coste (*m.*); costar (o:ue)

   —, insurance and freight (C.I.F.)   costo, seguro y flete (C.S.F.)

costly   costoso(a)

cotton   algodón (*m.*)

cough   tos (*f.*)

   — syrup   jarabe para la tos (*m.*)

count   contar (o:ue)

counter   mostrador (*m.*)

counterfeit bill   billete falso (*m.*)

country   país (*m.*)

county   condado (*m.*)

course   curso (*m.*)

cousin   primo(a) (*m., f.*)

cover   cubrir

coverage   cobertura (*f.*)

covered   cubierto(a)

crab   cangrejo (*m.*)

cracker   galleta (*f.*)

crazy   loco(a)

cream   crema (*f.*)

creation   creación (*f.*)

credit   crédito (*m.*); haber (*m.*); (*in college*) unidad (*f.*); acreditar

   — account   cuenta acreedora (*f.*)

   — card   tarjeta de crédito (*f.*)

   — document   instrumento de crédito (*m.*)

creditor   acreedor(a) (*m., f.*)

crime   délito (*m.*)

cross   cruzar

crutches   muletas (*f. pl.*)
cubic   cúbico(a)
cucumber   pepino (*m.*)
culture   cultura (*f.*)
cup   taza (*f.*)
currency   moneda (*f.*)
   — exchange office   casa de cambio (*f.*)
   — table   tabla de cotizaciones (*f.*)
current   actual, corriente
curtain   cortina (*f.*)
curve   curva (*f.*)
custard   flan (*m.*)
custom built   hecho(a) a la orden,
   construido(a) a la orden
customer   cliente (*m., f.*)
customs   aduana (*f.*)
   — form   declaración de aduana (*f.*)
cut   cortar
cylinder   cilindro (*m.*)

D

dad   papá (*m.*)
daily   al día, diariamente; (*adj.*) diario(a)
   — wage(s)   jornal (*m.*)
dairy store   lechería (*f.*)
damage (*to merchandise during transport*)
   avería (*f.*), **daño** (*m.*)
dance   baile (*m.*); bailar
danger   peligro (*m.*)
dangerous   peligroso(a)
dark-skinned   moreno(a)
data   datos (*m. pl.*)
   — base   base de datos (*f.*)

— **base management**   programa de manejo (administración) de base de datos (*m.*)

— **entry**   introducción de datos (*f.*)

date   fecha (*f.*)

daughter   hija (*f*)

day   día (*m.*)

— **after tomorrow**   pasado mañana

— **before yesterday**   anteayer

dead   muerto(a)

— **weight**   peso muerto (*m.*)

deal   oferta (*f.*); tratar

dear   querido(a)

death   muerte (*f.*)

debit   debe (*m.*); debitar

— **account**   cuenta deudora (*f.*)

debt   deuda (*f.*)

debtor   deudor(a) (*m., f.*)

decaffeinated   descafeinado(a)

December   diciembre

decide   decidir

decimeter   decímetro (*m.*)

declare   declarar

— **at fault**   declarar culpable

— **bankruptcy**   declararse en quiebra

— **oneself**   declararse

decrease   disminución (*f.*)

deduct   deducir

deductible   deducible

deduction   descuento (*m.*); deducción (*f.*)

deed   escritura (*f.*)

deep   hondo(a)

defeat   derrota (*f.*); vencer

defendant (criminal)   acusado(a) (*m., f.*); (*civil*) reo(a) (*m., f.*)

degree   grado (*m.*)
delay   demora (*f.*)
delicious   delicioso(a), rico(a), sabroso(a)
delight in   deleitarse
deliver   entregar
demand   exigir
deny   negar (e:ie)
deodorant   desodorante (*m.*)
department   departamento (*m.*)
— **store**   grandes almacenes (*m. pl.*)
departure   salida (*f.*)
depend (on)   depender (de)
dependent   dependiente (*m., f.*)
depending on   según
deposit   depositar
depositary   depositario(a)
depositor   depositante (*m., f.*)
depth (of a container)   alto (*m.*)
descend   bajar
describe   describir
design   diseño (*m.*); dibujo (*m.*); diseñar
designed   diseñado(a)
desk   escritorio (*m.*); buró (*m.*)
dessert   postre (*m.*)
destination   destino (*m.*)
detergent   detergente (*m.*)
detour   desvío (*m.*)
develop (film)   revelar
diabetes   diabetes (*f.*)
diabetic   diabético(a)
dial   marcar
diamond   brillante (*m.*), diamante (*m.*)
diarrhea   diarrea (*f.*)
die   morir (o:ue), fallecer

diet dieta (f.)
dietician dietista (f.)
difference diferencia (f.)
different distinto(a)
difficult difícil
difficulty dificultad (f.)
dimension medida (f.)
diminish rebajar
dining car coche comedor (m.)
dining room comedor (m.)
dinner cena (f.)
direct directo(a)
directly directamente
director director(a) (m., f.)
dirty sucio(a)
disability (disablement) invalidez (f.)
disappear desparecer
disaster desastre (m.)
discotheque discoteca (f.)
discount descuento (m.), rebaja (f.); descontar (o:ue)
discuss discutir
disease enfermedad (f.)
dish plato (m.)
dishwasher lavadora de platos (f.); lavaplatos (m.)
disinfect desinfectar
display window escaparate (m.), vidriera (f.)
distribute distribuir
district attorney fiscal (m., f.)
divide repartir
dividend dividendo (m.)
divorced divorciado(a)
dizziness mareo (m.)

dizzy mareado(a)
do hacer
  — **one (some) good** hacerle bien a uno
  — **(some) shopping** hacer (unas) compras
  — **the right thing** hacer bien
  — **well** irle bien a uno
doctor doctor(a)
  —'s **office** consultorio (*m.*)
document documento (*m.*)
dog perro(a) (*m., f.*)
dollar dólar (*m.*)
Dominican Republic República Dominicana
  (*f.*)
donate donar
donation donación (*f.*); donativo (*m.*)
door puerta (*f.*)
dormitory residencia universitaria (*f.*)
double doble (*m.*)
  — **bed** cama doble (*f.*), cama matrimonial (*f.*)
doubt dudar
down payment entrada (*f.*), cuota inicial (*f.*),
  enganche (*m.*) (*Méx.*)
downstairs planta baja (*f.*)
downtown centro de la ciudad (*m.*)
dozen docena (*f.*)
drawing dibujo (*m.*)
drawn girado(a)
dream sueño (*m.*)
dress vestido (*m.*); vestir(se) (e:i)
dresser cómoda (*f.*)
dressmaker modista (*m., f.*)
dressy de vestir
drink bebida (*f.*); tomar, beber
drive conducir, manejar

    — carefully manejar con cuidado
driver chofer (*m.*, *f.*), conductor(a) (*m.*, *f.*)
    —'s license licencia para conducir (manejar)
      (*f.*)
driving while intoxicated manejar bajo los
    efectos del alcohol
drop echar
drug medicina (*f.*); medicamento (*m.*)
drugstore farmacia (*f.*)
drunk borracho(a)
dry seco(a)
    — cleaner tintorería (*f.*)
dry-clean lavar en seco, limpiar en seco
dryer secadora (*f.*)
duck pato (*m.*)
due debido(a); vencido(a)
    — date fecha de vencimiento (*f.*)
during durante
dust the furniture sacudir los muebles
dustpan recogedor (*m.*)
duty (customs) derechos (*m. pl.*); aranceles (*m. pl.*); impuesto (*m.*)
    — free libre de derechos (impuestos)

E

each cada
ear (*inner*) oído (*m.*); (*outer*) oreja (*f.*)
early temprano
earn ganar
earnings ganancia (*f.*)
earring arete (*m.*)
earthquake terremoto (*m.*), temblor (*m.*)
easily fácilmente

east este (*m.*)
easy fácil
eat comer, tomar
economic(al) económico(a)
economics ciencias económicas (*f. pl.*)
edition edición (*f.*)
effective efectivo(a)
efficient eficiente
egg huevo (*m.*); blanquillo (*m.*) (*Méx.*)
eight ocho
eighty ochenta
either o, tampoco
elbow codo (*m.*)
electric eléctrico(a)
electrical outlet enchufe (*m.*)
electricity electricidad (*f.*)
electronic electrónico(a)
   — device equipo electrónico (*m.*)
   — mail (e-mail) correo electrónico (*m.*)
elegant elegante
elevator ascensor (*m.*), elevador (*m.*)
eleven once
eliminate eliminar
embrace abrazo (*m.*)
emergency emergencia (*f.*)
   — room sala de emergencia (*f.*)
emphasize hacer resaltar
employ contratar; emplear
employee empleado(a) (*m., f.*)
employer empleador(a) (*m., f.*); patrón(ona) (*m., f.*)
employment empleo (*m.*)
empty vacío(a); desocupado(a)
en route en ruta

enclosure anexo (*m.*); adjunto (*m.*)
end fin (*m.*); terminar
endowment insurance seguro dotal (*m.*)
engine motor (*m.*)
engineer ingeniero(a) (*m., f.*)
English inglés (*m.*)
enough bastante, suficiente
ensure asegurar
enter entrar
  — **(a market)** penetrar
  — **in the ledger** pasar al mayor
enterprise empresa (*f.*)
entertainment expenses gastos de
  representación (*m. pl.*)
entrust encargar
entry entrada (*f.*)
envelope sobre (*m.*)
equal to igual (que)
equipment equipo (*m.*)
equivalent equivalente
error error (*m.*)
escalator escalera rodante (*f.*), escalera
  mecánica (*f.*)
especially especialmente
espresso café expreso (*m.*), café solo (*m.*)
establishment establecimiento (*m.*)
estimate presupuesto (*m.*), estimado (*m.*)
evaluate evaluar
even though aunque
eventuality eventualidad (*f.*)
ever alguna vez
every cada; todo(a)
  — **day** todos los días
  — **two weeks** quincenal

everybody   todos(as)
everyone   todos(as)
everything   todo (*m.*)
exactly   exactamente, precisamente
exaggerate   exagerar
exam   examen (*m.*)
examination   examen (*m.*)
exceed   exceder
except   excepto
excess   exceso (*m.*)
  — **baggage**   exceso de equipaje (*m.*)
exchange   cambiar; cambio (*m.*)
  — **rate**   tasa de cambios (*f.*)
exclusion   exclusión (*f.*)
exclusive   exclusivo(a)
exclusively   exclusivamente
excursion   excursión (*f.*)
excuse me   perdón; con (su) permiso
executor   albacea (*m., f.*)
exemption   exención (*f.*)
exercise   ejercicio (*m.*); hacer ejercicio
exhaust pipe   tubo de escape (*m.*)
exhibition hall   salón de exhibición (*m.*)
exit   salida (*f.*)
expect   esperar
expel   expulsar
expenditure   egreso (*m.*)
expense   gasto (*m.*)
expensive   caro(a)
experience   experiencia (*f.*)
expert witness   experto(a) (*m., f.*), perito(a)
  (*m., f.*)
expiration date   fecha de vencimiento (*f.*)
explain   explicar

explanation   explicación (*f.*)
export   exportación (*f.*); exportar
express   expreso(a)
   — (train)   expreso (*m.*), rápido (*m.*)
expressway   autopista (*f.*)
exquisite   exquisito(a)
extend credit   conceder un crédito
exterior   exterior
   — (street) view   vista a la calle (*f.*)
extortion   extorsión (*f.*)
extra   extra
extract   extraer
eye   ojo (*m.*)
eyeglasses   anteojos (*m. pl.*), espejuelos (*f. pl.*), gafas (*f. pl.*), lentes (*m. pl.*)

F

fabric   tejido (*m.*); tela (*f.*)
facade   fachada (*f.*)
face   cara (*f.*)
   — (the street)   dar a (la calle)
facsimile   facsímil(e) (*m.*), fax (*m.*)
fair   equitativo(a)
fall down   caerse
family   familia (*f.*)
   — room   sala de estar (*f.*), salón de estar (*m.*)
fantastic   estupendo(a), fantástico(a)
far (from)   lejos (de)
fare   tarifa (*f.*)
fast   rápido(a)
fasten   abrocharse
   — one's seatbelt   abrocharse el cinturón
fat   gordo(a); grasa (*f.*)

father   padre (*m.*), papá (*m.*)
father-in-law   suegro (*m.*)
fax   facsímil(e) (*m.*), fax (*m.*)
fear   temer
feature   característica (*f.*)
February   febrero
federal   federal
fee   honorario (*m.*)
feed   alimentar
feel   sentir (e:ie)
  — pain   doler (o:ue)
felony   delito mayor (grave) (*m.*)
female flight attendant   azafata (*f.*)
fender   guardabarros (*m.*), guardafangos (*m.*)
fever   fiebre (*m.*)
few   pocos(as)
fiancé(e)   novio(a) (*m., f.*)
fiber   fibra (*f.*)
fifty   cincuenta
fight   pelea (*f.*)
file   registrar; archivador (*m.*)
  — a lawsuit   poner una demanda, demandar
filing cabinet   archivo (*m.*)
fill   llenar
  — out (a form)   llenar, rellenar
film   película (*f.*), filme (*m.*); filmar
final   final (*m.*)
finally   por fin; por último
financial   financiero(a)
  — statement   estado financiero (*m.*)
find   encontrar (o:ue)
  — out   averiguar
fine   bien; (*traffic*) multa (*f.*)
finger   dedo (*m.*)

finish acabar, terminar
fire incendio (*m.*), fuego (*m.*)
— **extinguisher** extinguidor de incendios
(*m.*)
fireman bombero (*m.*)
fireplace chimenea (*f.*)
firm firma (*f.*)
first primero(a); (*adv.*) primero
— **class** primera clase (*f.*)
— **day of classes** primer día de clases
— **degree murder** asesinato del primer
grado (*m.*)
— **floor** primer piso (*m.*)
fish pescado (*m.*); pescar
— **market** pescadería (*f.*)
fishing pole caña de pescar (*f.*)
fit caber; quedar
fitting room probador (*m.*)
five cinco
— **hundred** quinientos(as)
fix arreglar, reparar
fixed fijo(a)
— **rate** a plazo fijo
— **term (deposit)** a plazo fijo
fixtures enseres (*m. pl.*)
flat desinflado(a)
flight vuelo (*m.*)
— **attendant** auxiliar de vuelo (*m., f.*)
flood inundación (*f.*)
floor piso (*m.*), suelo (*m.*)
floppy disk drive disco flexible (*m.*)
flour harina (*f.*)
flower flor (*f.*)
— **shop** florería (*f.*)

fly volar (o:ue)
fold doblar
folio folio (*m.*)
follow resultar; seguir (e:i)
food comida (*f.*)
foot pie (*m.*)
football fútbol (*m.*)
for para, por, pues
   — **a specified time** a plazo fijo
   — **any reason** por cualquier motivo
   — **business reasons** por cuestiones de
     negocios
   — **personal use** para uso personal
   — **rent** se alquila
   — **sale** se vende
forbidden prohibido(a)
forecast pronóstico (*m.*)
forehead frente (*m.*)
foreigner extranjero(a) (*m., f.*)
forget olvidar(se) de
forgive perdonar
fork tenedor (*m.*)
form planilla (*f.*); forma (*f.*)
former anterior
fortunately afortunadamente
forty cuarenta
fourth cuarto(a)
fowl aves (*f. pl.*)
fracture fractura (*f.*); fracturar(se)
fragile frágil
fraud fraude (*m.*)
free gratis; libre
   — **on board (F.O.B.)** libre a bordo (L.A.B.)
freeway autopista (*f.*)

freight flete (*m.*)
French francés(a)
  — fries papas fritas (*f. pl.*)
  — toast pan francés (*m.*) (*Méx.*)
frequency (of business orders) asiduidad (*f.*)
fresh fresco(a)
  — foods alimentos frescos (*m. pl.*)
Friday viernes
fried frito(a)
friend amigo(a) (*m., f.*)
fringe benefit beneficio adicional (*m.*)
from de; desde
  — behind por detrás
  — one place to another de un lugar a otro
front: in — (of) frente (a)
  — desk recepción (*f.*)
frontier frontera (*f.*)
frozen congelado(a)
fruit fruta (*f.*)
  — store frutería (*f.*)
  — tree árbol frutal (*m.*)
fry freír (e:i)
frying pan sartén (*f.*)
full lleno(a); completo(a)
full-page a toda plana
full-time a tiempo completo
fun divertido(a)
  — to be with simpático(a)
function funcionar
funds fondos (*m. pl.*)
furnished amueblado(a)
furniture muebles (*m. pl.*)
  — factory or store mueblería (*f.*)
further más

future   futuro (*m.*)

G

gain weight   aumentar de peso, engordar
game   partido (*m.*)
garage   garaje (*m.*)
garden   jardín (*m.*)
garlic   ajo (*m.*)
garment   prenda de vestir (*f.*)
gasoline   gasolina (*f.*)
gate   puerta (*f.*)
gelatine   gelatina (*f.*)
general   general
   — **ledger**   (libro) mayor (*m.*)
   — **ledger entry**   pase al mayor (*m.*)
   — **manager**   gerente general (*m., f.*)
   — **partnership**   sociedad regular colectiva
   (*f.*)
generation   generación (*f.*)
generic   genérico(a)
gentleman   caballero (*m.*), señor (*m.*)
get   conseguir (e:i); obtener
   — **a grade**   sacar una nota
   — **a haircut**   cortarse el pelo
   — **better**   mejorarse
   — **bored**   aburrirse
   — **dressed**   vestir(se) (e:i)
   — **hurt**   lastimar(se)
   — **in**   subir
   — **married**   casarse
   — **off**   bajarse
   — **on**   subir
   — **rid of**   botar

    — **up** levantar(se)
    — **used to** acostumbrar(se)

gift regalo (*m.*)

gift-wrap envolver (o:ue) para regalo

girl chica (*f.*), muchacha (*f.*), niña (*f.*)

girlfriend novia (*f.*)

give dar
    — **a discount** descontar (o:ue)
    — **a gift** regalar
    — **(yourself) a shot** poner(se) una inyección
    — **a ticket** poner(se) una multa
    — **an account** rendir (e:i) informe
    — **back** devolver (o:ue)
    — **notice** avisar
    — **official authorization** acreditar
    — **someone a ride** llevar a alguien

glass copa (*f.*); vidrio (*m.*)

glove compartment portaguantes (*m.*)

go ir
    — **back** regresar
    — **bankrupt** quebrar (e:ie)
    — **by** pasar (por)
    — **down** bajar
    — **fishing** ir de pesca
    — **hunting** ir de caza
    — **in** entrar
    — **on a diet** poner(se) a dieta
    — **on a picnic** ir de picnic
    — **on a tour** ir de excursión
    — **out** salir
    — **shopping** ir de compras
    — **straight ahead** seguir (e:i) derecho
    — **through** pasar (por)
    — **to bed** acostar(se) (o:ue)

— **up** subir

gold oro (*m.*)

good bien (*m.*); (*adv.*) bueno; (*adj.*) buen(o)(a)

  — **afternoon.** Buenas tardes.

  — **appetite!** ¡Buen provecho!

  — **evening.** Buenas noches.

  — **morning (day).** Buenos días.

  — **night.** Buenas noches.

good-bye adiós

goods géneros (*m. pl.*); mercancías (*f. pl.*)

Gosh! ¡Caramba!

government gobierno (*m.*)

gown bata (*f.*)

grade nota (*f.*)

  — **point average (GPA)** promedio de notas (*m.*)

graduate graduarse

graduation graduación (*f.*)

grandfather abuelo (*m.*)

grandmother abuela (*f.*)

grape uva (*f.*)

grapefruit toronja (*f.*)

graphic gráfico (*m.*)

grass césped (*m.*); zacate (*m.*) (*Méx.*)

great estupendo(a), magnífico(a)

green verde

  — **card** tarjeta verde (*f.*)

  — **grocery** verdulería (*f.*)

  — **salad** ensalada de lechuga (*f.*)

greet saludar

grey gris

grilled asado(a)

grind moler (o:ue)

gross bruto(a)

— **income**   ingreso bruto (*m.*)
— **profit**   utilidad bruta (*f.*)
— **weight**   peso bruto (*m.*)
ground   suelo (*m.*)
  floor   planta baja (*f.*)
— **meat**   carne picada (molida) (*f.*), picadillo (*m.*)
group insurance   seguro de grupo (*m.*); seguro colectivo (*m.*)
grouper   mero (*m.*)
grow   crecer
guarantee   garantía (*f.*)
guardian   tutor(a) (*m., f.*)
guest   huésped (*m., f.*), invitado(a) (*m., f.*)
— **room**   cuarto de huéspedes (*m.*)
guilt   culpa (*f.*)
guilty   culpable
  not —   inocente
gymnasium   gimnasio (*m.*)

H

Ha!   ¡Ja!
habit   hábito (*m.*)
hair   pelo (*m.*)
— **dryer**   secador (*m.*)
hairdresser   peluquero(a) (*m., f.*)
half   medio(a); mitad (*f.*)
— **an hour**   media hora
hall(way)   pasillo (*m.*)
ham   jamón (*m.*)
hamburger   hamburguesa (*f.*)
hand   mano (*f.*)

handbag bolso(a) (*m., f.*); bolso de mano (*m.*); cartera (*f.*); maletín de mano (*m.*)

handicraft artesanía (*f.*)

handkerchief pañuelo (*m.*)

handsome guapo(a)

happen ocurrir, pasar, suceder

happy feliz

hard drive disco duro (*m.*)

hard-boiled egg huevo duro (*m.*)

hardly apenas

hardware (computer) soporte físico (*m.*)
   — **store** ferretería (*f.*)

haste prisa (*f.*)

have tener
   — **a collision** chocar
   — **a good time** divertirse (e:ie)
   — **a seat** tomar asiento
   — **available** ofrecer
   — **breakfast** desayunar
   — **fun** divertirse (e:ie)
   — **just done (something)** acabar de (+ *inf.*)
   — **lunch** almorzar (o:ue)
   — **something to declare** tener algo que declarar
   — **supper (dinner)** cenar
   — **to** deber; tener que (+ *inf.*)

he él (*m.*)

head cabeza (*f.*)
   — **of household (of the family)** cabeza de familia (*m., f.*), jefe(a) de familia (*m., f.*)

health salud (*f.*)
   — **insurance** seguro de salud (*m.*)

hearing oído (*m.*)

heart corazón (*m.*)

heating calefacción (*f.*)
height alto (*m.*), altura (*f.*)
heir heredero(a) (*m., f.*)
Hello. Hola.
   say — saludar
help ayudar; ayuda (*f.*)
   Help! ¡Auxilio!, ¡Socorro!
her su(s)
here aquí
   —'s ... aquí tiene...
hers suyo(a)(os)(as)
herself ella misma
Hi. Hola.
high alto(a)
highway carretera (*f.*)
hip cadera (*f.*)
hire contratar, emplear
his su(s); suyo(a)(os)(as)
hit pegar
   — oneself golpearse
hold tener; (*a position*) desempeñar
home casa (*f.*), hogar (*m.*)
homemade casero(a)
honeymoon luna de miel (*f.*)
hood capó (*m.*)
hope esperar
   I — ... Ojalá...
horn bocina (*f.*), claxon (*m.*), pito (*m.*)
horoscope horóscopo (*m.*)
horse caballo (*m.*)
hospital hospital (*m.*)
hot caliente
hotel hotel (*m.*)
hour hora (*f.*)

house casa (*f.*)
housing vivienda (*f.*)
how? ¿cómo?
— **are you?** ¿Cómo está Ud.?
— **are you doing?** ¿Qué tal?
— **do you do?** Mucho gusto.
— **far?** ¿A qué distancia?
— **far in advance?** ¿Con cuánta anticipación?
— **is it going?** ¿Qué tal?
— **long?** ¿Cuánto tiempo?
— **many?** ¿Cuántos(as)?
— **may I (we) help you?** ¿En qué puedo (podemos) servirle?
— **much?** ¿Cuánto?
— **much is it?** ¿Cuánto(a) es?
— **tall are you?** ¿Cuánto mide Ud.?
How . . . ! ¡Qué... !
hug abrazo (*m.*)
human humano(a)
hundred ciento (*m.*)
hunger hambre (*f.*)
hurricane huracán (*m.*)
hurry darse prisa
— **up** apurarse
hurt doler (o:ue)
husband esposo (*m.*)
hygienic higiénico(a)

I

I yo
— **(already) know it.** Ya lo sé.
— **believe it!** ¡Ya lo creo!

— **hope so.**   Ojalá que sí.
—**'ll say!**   ¡Ya lo creo!
—**'ll see you later.**   Hasta luego.
—**'m coming.**   Ya voy.
—**'m sorry.**   Lo siento.
ice cream   helado (*m.*)
ice pack   bolsa de hielo (*f.*)
idea   idea (*f.*)
identification (I.D.)   identificación (*f.*)
if   si
— **only . . .**   Ojalá...
— **possible**   si es posible
imagine   figurarse
immigration   inmigración (*f.*)
import   importar
important   importante
— **thing(s)**   lo importante
imported   importado(a)
importer   importador(a) (*m., f.*)
improve   mejorar; (*health*) mejorarse
in   dentro de, en
— **accordance (with)**   de acuerdo (con)
— **addition**   por otra parte
— **advance**   por adelantado
— **all**   en total
— **any case**   de todos modos
— **case**   en caso de que
— **cash**   en efectivo
— **deposit**   en fondo; en depósito
— **equal parts**   a partes iguales
— **excess (of)**   en exceso (de)
— **love**   enamorado(a)
— **order**   en regla
— **order to**   para; para que

— **other words**   es decir
— **spite of the fact that**   a pesar de que
— **stock**   en existencia
— **that case**   entonces
— **the back**   al fondo
— **the meantime**   mientras tanto
— **the morning**   por la mañana
inch   pulgada (*f.*)
include   incluir
included   incluido(a)
including   incluido(a)
income   ingreso (*m.*), renta (*f.*)
inconvenience   inconveniente (*m.*)
increase   aumento (*m.*); aumentar
indeed   en realidad
indemnification   indemización (*f.*)
indicate   indicar, marcar
individual   individual
— **retirement account (I.R.A.)**   cuenta
   individual de retiro (*f.*)
industry   industria (*f.*)
inexpensive   barato(a)
infection   infección (*f.*)
influence   influencia (*f.*)
inform   avisar
information   datos (*m. pl.*); información (*f.*);
   informes (*m. pl.*)
inheritance   herencia (*f.*)
initial   inicial (*f.*)
injury   lesión (*f.*)
inside   adentro
insolvency   insolvencia (*f.*)
insolvent   insolvente
inspect   inspeccionar

inspection inspección (f.)
inspector inspector(a) (m., f.)
installed instalado(a)
instant instantáneo(a)
institution institución (f.)
instrument instrumento (m.)
insurance seguro (m.)
  — company asegurador(a) (m., f.)
insure asegurar
insured asegurado(a) (m., f.)
intelligent inteligente
intend (to do something) pensar (e:ie) (+ inf.)
intention propósito (m.)
intercom intercomunicador (m.)
interest interés (m.); interesar
  — rate tipo de interés (m.), tasa de interés (f.)
interested interesado(a)
interior interior
  — view vista interior (f.)
international internacional
Internet Internet (f.); red (f.)
interpreter intérprete (m., f.)
intersection intersección (f.)
  — of la esquina de
interview entrevista (f.)
intestate intestado(a)
  — case abintestato (m.)
introduce introducir
inventory inventario (m.), existencias (f. pl.)
invest invertir (e:i)
invested invertido(a)
investigate investigar
investment inversión (f.)
  — officer asesor(a) de inversiones (m., f.)

invitation   invitación (*f.*)
invite   invitar
invited   invitado(a)
invoice   factura (*f.*)
iron (clothing)   plancha (*f.*); planchar
issue   edición (*f.*)
issuer   país que lo expide (*m.*)
It doesn't matter.   No importa.
It doesn't work.   No funciona.
it is necessary to   hay que
it's: — (+ *time*)   es (son) la(s) (+ *time*)
   — no good.   No sirve.
   — nothing.   De nada.
   — out of order.   No funciona.
   — true.   Es verdad.
   — useless.   No sirve.
item   artículo (*m.*)
itinerary   itinerario (*m.*)

J

jack   gato (*m.*)
jacket   chaqueta (*f.*); chamarra (*f.*) (*Méx.*)
jam   jalea (*f.*)
January   enero
jewelry store   joyería (*f.*)
job   puesto (*m.*), posición (*f.*), empleo (*m.*)
   — description   descripción del contenido de
     trabajo (*f.*)
joint account   cuenta conjunta (*f.*)
joke   broma (*f.*); decir algo en broma
jot down   anotar
journal   (libro) diario (*m.*)
   — entry   asiento de diario (*m.*)

judge   juez (*m., f.*)
juice   jugo (*m.*)
July   julio
June   junio
jury   jurado (*m.*)
just a moment   un momento
just in case   por si acaso
just me   yo solo(a)

K

keep   mantener; quedarse (con)
   — the books   llevar la contabilidad
kept   cuidado(a)
key   llave (*f.*); (*on keyboard*) tecla (*f.*); (*into a computer*) registrar
keyboard   teclado (*m.*)
kid   decir algo en broma
kilo(gram)   kilo (*m.*), kilogramo (*m.*)
kilometer   kilómetro (*m.*)
kind   amable, bueno(a)
kiosk   kiosco (*m.*), quiosco (*m.*)
kitchen   cocina (*f.*)
   — sink   fregadero (*m.*)
klaxon   bocina (*f.*), claxon (*m.*)
knapsack   mochila (*f.*)
knee   rodilla (*f.*)
knockout (boxing)   nocaut (*m.*)
know   saber; conocer
   I —.   Ya lo sé.

L

label   etiqueta (*f.*)

labor   mano de obra (*f.*)

lack   hacer falta

ladder   escalera de mano (*f.*)

ladies clothing   ropa para damas (*f.*)

lady   dama (*f.*), señora (*f.*), señorita (*f.*)

lake   lago (*m.*)

lamb   cordero (*m.*)

lamp   lámpara (*f.*)

land   tierra (*f.*); (*a plane*) aterrizar
   — **transportation**   transporte por tierra (*m.*)

landscape   paisaje (*m.*)

language   lengua (*f.*), idioma (*m.*)
   — **laboratory**   laboratorio de lenguas (*m.*)

lap table   mesita (*f.*)

laptop computer   computador(a) portátil (*m.*,
   f.), ordenador portátil (*m.*)

large   grande

last (a length of time)   demorar; durar; (*adj.*)
   pasado(a), (*in a series*) último(a)
   — **name**   apellido (*m.*)
   — **name (maternal)**   apellido materno (*m.*)
   — **name (paternal)**   apellido paterno (*m.*)
   — **night**   anoche

lastly   por último

late   tarde

later   al rato, después de, luego, más tarde

Latin America   Latinoamérica

Latin American   latinoamericano(a)

laundry room   cuarto de lavar (*m.*)

law   ley (*f.*)
   — **office**   bufete (*m.*)

lawn   césped (*m.*); zacate (*m.*) (*Méx.*)

lawsuit   demanda (*f.*), pleito (*m.*)

lawyer   abogado(a) (*m., f.*)

learn   aprender
lease   arrendamiento (*m.*); alquilar, arrendar
least   menos
leather   cuero (*m.*)
leave   salir
   — **(behind)**   dejar
   — **much to be desired**   dejar mucho que
      desear
left   izquierda (*f.*)
leg   pierna (*f.*)
legal   legal
lemon   limón (*m.*)
lemonade   limonada (*f.*)
lend   prestar
lender   prestamista (*m., f.*)
length   largo (*m.*)
less   menos
   — **than**   menos de; menor
lessee   arrendatario(a) (*m., f.*)
let   dejar
   —**'s see**   a ver
letter   carta (*f.*)
   — **of recommendation**   carta de
      recomendación (*f.*)
   — **opener**   abrecartas (*m.*)
letterhead   membrete (*m.*)
lettuce   lechuga (*f.*)
level   nivel (*m.*)
liabilities   pasivo (*m.*)
liability   responsabilidad civil (*f.*)
library   biblioteca (*f.*)
license   licencia (*f.*)
   — **plate**   chapa (*f.*), placa (*f.*)

life vida (*f.*)
  — **annuity** renta vitalicia (*f.*)
  — **expectancy** probabilidad de vida (*f.*)
  — **insurance** seguro de vida (*m.*)
  — **preserver** salvavidas (*m.*)
lift weights levantar pesas
light luz (*f.*); lámpara (*f.*)
lightweight (boxing) peso ligero (*m.*)
like gustar
  — **this (that)** así
limit límite (*m.*)
Limited Liability Company Sociedad de responsabilidad limitada (S.R.L.) (*f.*)
line línea (*f.*); fila (*f.*)
  — **of business** giro (*m.*)
  — **of merchandise** renglón (*m.*)
linoleum linóleo (*m.*)
liquid líquido (*m.*)
liquidate liquidar
liquidity liquidez (*f.*)
list lista (*f.*)
listen (to) escuchar
  Listen! ¡Oye!
literature literatura (*f.*)
litigation pleito (*m.*)
litter tirar basura
little chico(a), pequeño(a); (*quantity*) poco(a)
  a — un poco
live vivir
  — **animal** animal vivo (*m.*)
living room sala (*f.*)
load cargamento (*m.*), carga (*f.*); cargar
loan préstamo (*m.*)
lobby vestíbulo (*m.*)

lobster langosta (*f.*)
local local
locked inmovilizado(a)
logo logo(grama) (*m.*)
long largo(a)
   — **distance** larga distancia (*f.*)
look mirar
   — **at oneself** mirarse
   — **for** buscar
   — **like** parecer
lose perder (e:ie)
   — **consciousness** perder el conocimiento
   — **weight** adelgazar
loss pérdida (*f.*)
lost cause un caso perdido
loudspeaker altavoz (*m.*), altoparlante (*m.*)
love amor; encantarle a uno; querer (e:ie)
low bajo(a)
lube and oil change engrase (*m.*)
lubrication engrase (*m.*), lubricación (*f.*)
luck suerte (*f.*)
luckily afortunadamente, por suerte
luggage equipaje (*m.*)
lunch almuerzo (*m.*); comida (*f.*)

M

M.D. doctor(a) (*m.*, *f.*)
Ma'am señora (*f.*)
machine máquina (*f.*)
Madam señora (*f.*)
magazine revista (*f.*)
   — **stand** kiosco (*m.*), puesto de revistas (*m.*),
      quiosco (*m.*)

magnificent magnífico(a)

mail echar al correo; correspondencia (*f.*), correo (*m.*)

— **carrier** cartero(a) (*m., f.*)

mailbox buzón (*m.*)

main office casa matriz (*f.*)

maintain mantener

majority (of) mayoría (de) (*f.*), mayor parte (de) (*f.*)

make hacer; confeccionar

— **a deal** llegar a un arreglo

— **a decision** tomar una decisión

— **a stopover** hacer escala

— **an appointment** pedir (e:i) turno

— **plans** hacer planes

— **reservations** hacer reservaciones

— **the bed** hacer la cama

makeup maquillaje (*m.*)

mall centro comercial (*m.*)

man hombre (*m.*)

manage administrar

manager encargado(a) (*m., f.*), gerente (*m., f.*)

manslaughter homicidio no premeditado (*m.*)

manufacture fabricación (*f.*); fabricar, producir

manufactured fabricado(a)

manufacturer's trademark marca de fábrica (*f.*)

manufacturing (*adj.*) manufacturero(a)

many muchos(as)

map mapa (*m.*)

March marzo

margarine margarina (*f.*)

marital status estado civil (*m.*)

mark marcar
marked marcado(a)
market mercado (*m.*)
marmalade mermelada (*f.*)
married casado(a)
— **couple** matrimonio (*m.*)
marvelous maravilloso(a)
mashed potatoes puré de papas (*m.*)
massive masivo(a)
master bedroom cuarto principal (*m.*)
match partido (*m.*)
material material (*m.*)
mathematics matemáticas (*f. pl.*)
matter importar
maximum máximo(a)
May mayo
maybe a lo mejor, quizás
mayonnaise mayonesa (*f.*)
meal comida (*f.*)
means medios (*m. pl.*); capacidad (*f.*)
— **of payment** forma de pago (*f.*)
— **of transportation** medios de transporte
    (*m. pl.*)
measure medir (e:i); medida (*f.*)
measurement medida (*f.*)
meat carne (*f.*)
— **market** carnicería (*f.*)
meatball albóndiga (*f.*)
mechanic mecánico(a)
mechanic's shop taller de reparaciones (*m.*)
medical médico(a)
— **and hospital care** atención médica y
    hospitalaria (*f.*)
— **doctor** doctor(a) (*m., f.*)

— **insurance**   seguro médico (*m.*)

medicine   medicina (*f.*), medicamento (*m.*)

medium   mediano(a)

— **height**   de estatura mediana

meet   encontrar (o:ue)

meeting   junta (*f.*), reunión (*f.*)

member   miembro (*m.*)

memorandum   memorando (*m.*)

memory   memoria (*f.*)

mention   mencionar

menu   menú (*m.*)

merchandise   mercancía (*f.*), mercadería (*f.*)

message   mensaje (*m.*)

meter   metro (*m.*)

Mexican   mexicano(a)

Mexico   México

microchip   pastilla (*f.*)

microwave   microonda (*f.*)

midnight   medianoche (*f.*)

midterm exam   examen parcial (*m.*)

mile   milla (*f.*)

mileage   millaje (*m.*)

milk   leche (*f.*)

mineral   mineral (*m.*)

— **water**   agua mineral (*f.* but **el agua
   mineral**)

minimum   mínimo (*m.*)

minor   menor de edad (*m., f.*)

minute   minuto (*m.*)

— **book**   libro de actas (*m.*)

miracle   milagro (*m.*)

mirror   espejo (*m.*)

miscellaneous expenses   gastos varios (*m. pl.*)

miscellany   miscelánea (*f.*)

misdemeanor   delito menor (*m.*), delito menos grave (*m.*)

Miss   señorita (Srta.) (*f.*)

mixed   mixto(a)

model   modelo (*m.*), típico(a)

modem   módem (*m.*)

modern   moderno(a)

modernize   modernizar

mom   mamá (*f.*)

moment   momento (*m.*)

Monday   lunes (*m.*)

money   dinero (*m.*), moneda (*f.*)

   — exchange office   oficina de cambio (*f.*)

   — market account   cuenta del mercado de dinero (*f.*)

   — order   giro postal (*m.*)

moneygram   giro telegráfico (*m.*)

monitor   monitor (*m.*)

month   mes (*m.*)

monthly   (*adj.*) mensual; (*adv.*) al mes

   — payment   mensualidad (*f.*)

   — salary   sueldo mensual (*m.*)

monument   monumento (*m.*)

more   más

   — or less   más o menos

morning   mañana (*f.*)

mortgage   hipoteca (*f.*)

most   la mayor parte (*f.*)

mostly   principalmente

mother   madre (*f.*), mamá (*f.*)

mother-in-law   suegra (*f.*)

motor   motor (*m.*)

motorcycle   motocicleta (moto) (*f.*)

mountain   montaña (*f.*)

mouse   ratón (*m.*)
moustache   bigote (*m.*)
mouth   boca (*f.*)
move   (*relocate*) mudarse, trasladar
movie   película (*f.*)
Mr.   señor (Sr.) (*m.*)
Mrs.   señora (Sra.) (*f.*)
much   mucho(a)
muffler   silenciador (*m.*)
municipal   municipal
museum   museo (*m.*)
musical   musical
musician   músico(a) (*m., f.*)
must   deber
mustard   mostaza (*f.*)
mutual fund   fondo mutuo (*m.*)
my   mi(s)

N

name   nombre (*m.*); nombrar
   in my —   a nombre mío, en mi nombre
   my — is . . .   me llamo...
   sender's company —   antefirma (*f.*)
nap   siesta (*f.*)
napkin   servilleta (*f.*)
narrow   angosto(a)
national   nacional
nationality   nacionalidad (*f.*)
native   nativo(a)
natural phenomenon   fenómeno natural (*m.*),
   fuerza mayor (*f.*)
nausea   náusea (*f.*)
near   cercano(a); cerca (de)

necessary   necesario(a)
  — things   lo necesario
necessity   necesidad (f.)
neck   cuello (m.)
need   necesidad (f.); hacer falta, necesitar
needed   necesario(a)
negociate   negociar
neighbor   vecino(a) (m., f.)
neighborhood   barrio (m.), vecindario (m.)
neither   ni; tampoco; ni... tampoco
nervous   nervioso(a)
net   neto(a)
  — profit   utilidad neta (f.)
  — weight   peso neto (m.)
never   nunca
nevertheless   sin embargo
new   nuevo(a)
newly   recién
news   noticia(s) (f.)
newspaper   diario (m.), periódico (m.)
next   próximo(a)
  — day   al día siguiente
  — to   al lado de
nice   bueno(a), simpático(a)
night   noche (f.)
  — stand (table)   mesa de noche (f.), mesita de
    noche (f.)
nine   nueve
nineteen   diecinueve
ninety   noventa
no   no
  — longer   ya no
  — one   nadie
  — smoking   no fumar

nobody nadie
noise ruido (*m.*)
none ningún(o)(a)
noodle fideo (*m.*)
noon mediodía (*m.*)
nor ni
normal normal
north norte (*m.*)
North American norteamericano(a)
  — Free Trade Agreement (NAFTA)
    Tratado de Libre Comercio de América del
    Norte (TLCAN) (*m.*)
northeast noreste (*m.*)
northwest noroeste (*m.*)
nose nariz (*f.*)
not no
  — either ni... tampoco
  — guilty inocente (*m., f.*)
notably notablemente
note anotar
nothing nada
  — else nada más
noun nombre (*m.*)
novel novela (*f.*)
November noviembre
now ahora; ahorita (*Méx.*)
number número (*m.*)
nurse enfermero(a) (*m., f.*)
nut nuez (*f.*)

O

object objeto (*m.*)
obsolete obsoleto(a)

obtain obtener, conseguir (e:i)
occupation ocupación (*f.*)
occupied (a house) habitado(a)
occur ocurrir
October octubre
of de
  — **age** mayor de edad
  — **course** cómo no, desde luego
offense delito (*m.*)
offer oferta (*f.*)
office oficina (*f.*)
  — **clerk** oficinista (*m., f.*)
officer on duty oficial de guardia (*m., f.*)
oil aceite (*m.*), petróleo (*m.*)
  — **change** cambio de aceite (*m.*)
okay (*adv.*) bueno
old viejo(a)
older mayor
olive aceituna (*f.*)
olive-skinned moreno(a)
omelet tortilla (*f.*)
  — **with potatoes** tortilla a la española (*f.*)
on en; por; sobre
  — **behalf of** a favor de
  — **foot** a pie
  — **one's account** ir por su cuenta
  — **the dot (time)** en punto
  — **the way here (there)** para acá (allá)
  — **time** a tiempo
  — **top of** sobre
  turned — **(a light)** encendido(a)
one uno(a)
  — **moment** un momento
  — **must** hay que

—'s suyo(a)(os)(as)

one-way ticket pasaje de ida (*m.*), billete de ida (*m.*)

only solamente, sólo, únicamente

  — child hijo(a) único(a) (*m., f.*)

  — one único(a)

  the — thing lo único

open abierto(a); abrir

operate operar; manejar

operating system sistema operativo (*m.*)

operation operación (*f.*)

operator operador(a) (*m., f.*)

optimist optimista (*m., f.*)

option opción (*f.*)

or o

orange naranja (*f.*)

  — juice jugo de naranja (*m.*)

orchestra orquesta (*f.*)

order orden (*m.*), pedido (*m.*); pedir (e:i), ordenar

organ órgano (*m.*)

organize organizar

origin origen (*m.*), procedencia (*f.*)

other otro(a)

others: the — los(las) demás

Ouch! ¡Ay!

our nuestro(a)(os)(as)

ours el (la) (los) (las) nuestro(a)(os)(as)

out afuera

  — of order descompuesto(a)

outfit conjunto (*m.*)

outside afuera; por fuera

oven horno (*m.*)

over sobre

  — there allá; por allá

overdraft   sobregiro (*m.*)
overdrawn check   cheque sin fondos (*m.*)
overhead expenses   gastos generales (*m. pl.*)
overheat   recalentarse (e:ie)
overlook the street   dar a la calle
overtime   tiempo extra (*m.*)
owe   deber
own a house   tener casa propia
owner   dueño(a) (*m., f.*), propietario(a) (*m., f.*)
oyster   ostra (*f.*)

P

pack   cajetilla (*f.*)
package   bulto (*m.*), cajetilla (*f.*), paquete (*m.*)
packing   embalaje (*m.*)
page (accounting books)   folio (*m.*)
pain   dolor (*m.*)
paint   pintar; pintura (*f.*)
painted   pintado(a)
painter   pintor(a) (*m., f.*)
pair   par (*m.*)
pajama   pijama (*m.*)
pants   pantalones (*m. pl.*)
pantsuit   conjunto de pantalón y chaqueta (*m.*)
pantyhose   pantimedia(s) (*f.*)
paper   papel (*m.*)
   — clip   sujetapapeles (*m.*)
Pardon me.   Perdón.
parents   padres (*m. pl.*)
park   (*a car*) estacionar, aparcar; parque (*m.*)
parking   estacionamiento (*m.*)
   — lot   zona de estacionamiento (*f.*),
     estacionamiento (*m.*)

— **meter** parquímetro (*m.*)

part parte (*f.*), pieza (*f.*)

participate participar

participation participación (*f.*)

partner socio(a) (*m., f.*)

part-time medio tiempo; a medio día

party fiesta (*f.*); parte (*f.*)

— **pooper** aguafiestas (*m., f.*)

pass pasar

— **the time** pasar el tiempo

passenger pasajero(a) (*m., f.*)

passer-by transeúnte (*m., f.*)

passing by que pasa

passport pasaporte (*m.*)

past pasado(a)

patent patente (*f.*)

patience paciencia (*f.*)

patio patio (*m.*)

pavement pavimento (*m.*)

pawnbroker prestamista (*m., f.*)

pay pagar

— **attention** hacer caso

— **in advance** adelantar

— **in cash** pagar al contado

— **in installments** pagar a plazos

— **off** liquidar

payroll nómina (*f.*)

peach durazno (*m.*), melocotón (*m.*)

peanut cacahuate (*m.*) (*Méx.*), maní (*m.*)

pear pera (*f.*)

peas arvejas (*f. pl.*), chícharos (*m. pl.*), guisantes (*m. pl.*)

pedestrian peatón(ona) (*m., f.*)

peel pelar

pen   pluma (*f.*)
penalty   multa (*f.*)
pencil   lápiz (*m.*)
penetrate   penetrar
penicillin   penicilina (*f.*)
pension   pensión (*f.*)
people   gente (*f.*)
pepper   pimienta (*f.*)
per   por
— **day**   por día
— **unit**   por unidad
percent   por ciento
perfume and toiletry shop   perfumería (*f.*)
perhaps   a lo mejor, quizás
periodically   periódicamente
peripheral (device)   periférico (*m.*)
permanent (wave)   permanente (*f.*)
permit   permiso (*m.*)
person   persona (*f.*)
— **in charge (of)**   encargado(a) (*m., f.*)
personal   personal
— **property**   bienes muebles (*m. pl.*)
personalized   personalizado(a)
personnel   personal (*m.*)
pet   animalito (*m.*)
petty cash   caja (*f.*)
pharmacy   farmacia (*f.*)
phone   teléfono (*m.*)
— **book**   guía de teléfonos (*f.*), directorio telefónico (*m.*)
— **number**   número de teléfono (*m.*)
photo   foto (*f.*)
photocopier   fotocopiadora (*f.*)
photograph   fotografía (*f.*)

photography fotografía (*f.*)
physics física (*f.*)
pick up recoger
picnic picnic (*m.*)
pie pastel (*m.*)
piece pedazo (*m.*), trozo (*m.*)
  — of toast tostada (*f.*)
pill pastilla (*f.*)
pillow almohada (*f.*)
pillowcase funda (*f.*)
pilot piloto (*m., f.*)
pineapple piña (*f.*)
pink rosado(a)
pitcher jarra (*f.*)
pity lástima (*f.*)
  it's a — es una lástima
place lugar (*m.*); poner
  — an order hacer un pedido
  — of birth lugar de nacimiento (*m.*)
  — of interest lugar de interés (*m.*)
plain omelet tortilla a la francesa (*f.*)
plan plan (*m.*); pensar (e:ie), planear
plane avión (*m.*)
plantain plátano (*m.*)
plate plato (*m.*)
platform (railway) andén (*m.*)
play jugar (u:ue)
  — a sport jugar un deporte
plaza plaza (*f.*)
please favor de; por favor; sírvase
Pleased to meet you. Mucho gusto (en conocerle).
pleasure agrado (*m.*)
plug in enchufar

plus más
pocket calculator calculadora de bolsillo (*f.*)
police (department) policía (*f.*)
— **news** noticias policiales (*f. pl.*)
— **officer** policía (*m., f.*)
policy póliza (*f.*)
— **holder** asegurado(a) (*m., f.*),
    subscriptor(a) (*m., f.*)
poll sondeo de la opinión pública (*m.*)
poor thing pobrecito(a) (*m., f.*)
popular popular
pork puerco (*m.*); cerdo (*m.*)
portable portátil
porter maletero(a) (*m., f.*)
position puesto (*m.*); posición (*f.*)
— **held** puesto desempeñado (*m.*)
positive positivo(a)
possession posesión (*f.*)
possible posible
post puesto (*m.*); posición (*f.*)
— **office** oficina de correos (*f.*)
— **office box** apartado postal (*m.*), casilla de
    correo (*f.*)
postage franqueo (*m.*); porte (*m.*)
— **due** porte debido
— **paid** porte pagado
postcard tarjeta postal (*f.*)
poster cartel (*m.*)
postmark matasellos (*m.*)
postscript posdata (*f.*)
pot olla (*f.*)
potato papa (*f.*), patata (*f.*)
pottery alfarería (*f.*)
— **shop (factory)** alfarería (*f.*)

poultry   aves (*f. pl.*)
pound   libra (*f.*)
powder   polvo (*m.*)
powerful   poderoso(a)
practice   practicar
preceded   precedido(a)
precisely   precisamente
prefer   preferir (e:ie)
preferable   preferible
pregnant   embarazada
premeditated   premeditado(a)
premium   prima (*f.*)
prepaid response   contestación pagada (*f.*)
prepare   preparar, confeccionar
prescribe   recetar
present   (*adj.*) actual; presentar
presentation   presentación (*f.*)
presently   actualmente
president   presidente (*m., f.*)
pretty   bonito(a), lindo(a)
previous   anterior
price   precio (*m.*), importe (*m.*)
pride   orgullo (*m.*)
principally   principalmente
print   imprimir; letra de molde (*f.*)
printed matter   impreso (*m.*)
printer   impresor(a) (*m., f.*)
printing   impresión (*f.*), letra de molde (*f.*)
private   privado(a)
prize   premio (*m.*)
problem   problema (*m.*)
procedure   trámite (*m.*)
product   producto (*m.*)

professional profesional (*m., f.*); profesionalista (*m., f.*)

professor profesor(a) (*m., f.*)

profit ganancia (*f.*); utilidad (*f.*)
   — and loss statement estado de pérdidas y ganancias (*m.*)

program programa (*m.*)

programmer programador(a) (*m., f.*)

prohibited prohibido(a)

prolong prolongar

promissory note (I.O.U.) pagaré (*m.*)

proof (written) comprobante (*m.*); prueba (*f.*); constancia (*f.*)

property propiedad (*f.*)
   — tax impuesto a la propiedad (*m.*)

prosecutor abogado(a) acusador(a) (*m., f.*)

prosperous próspero(a)

protein proteína (*f.*)

provided that con tal que

provider proveedor(a) (*m., f.*), suministrador(a) (*m., f.*)

proximity proximidad (*f.*)

public público(a)

publicity publicidad (*f.*), propaganda (*f.*)

publish publicar

pudding budín (*m.*)

pull over (a car) arrimar (el carro)

purchase compra (*f.*); comprar
   — and sale agreement compraventa (*f.*)
   — order orden de compra (*f.*); pedido (*m.*)
   — price precio de compra (*m.*)

purchasing manager jefe(a) de compras (*m., f.*)

purple morado(a)

purse bolsa (*f.*); cartera (*f.*)

put poner
- **— in a cast** enyesar
- **— on** ponerse
- **— out (a fire)** apagar
- **— to bed** acostar(se) (o:ue)
- **— together** confeccionar
- **— up for sale** poner a la venta

Q

qualification calificación (*f.*)
qualify calificar
quality calidad (*f.*)
quantity cantidad (*f.*)
quarter trimestre (*m.*)
question pregunta (*f.*)
quite bastante

R

race raza (*f.*)
radiator radiador (*m.*)
radio radio (*f.*)
railroad ferrocarril (*m.*), tren (*m.*)
- **— station** estación de trenes (*f.*)

rain llover (o:ue); lluvia (*f.*)
rainshower aguacero (*m.*)
raise levantar(se); aumento (*m.*)
rape violación (*f.*)
raped violado(a)
rare crudo(a)
rate tarifa (*f.*)
raw material materia prima (*f.*)
razor máquina de afeitar (*f.*)

   — blade   navajita (*f.*)
reach   alcanzar
   — an agreement   llegar a un arreglo
read   leer
ready   listo(a)
real estate   bienes inmuebles (*m. pl.*); inmuebles
   (*m. pl.*); bienes raíces (*m. pl.*)
   — agent   corredor(a) de bienes raíces (*m., f.*)
   — tax   contribución (*f.*)
reason   motivo (*m.*)
reasonable   equitativo(a), razonable
receipt   recibo (*m.*), comprobante (*m.*)
receive   recibir
received   recibido(a)
receiver   depositario(a) (*m., f.*)
recently   recientemente; recién
reception desk   recepción (*f.*)
receptionist   recepcionista (*m., f.*)
recipient   destinatario(a) (*m., f.*)
recline   reclinar
recommend   recomendar (e:ie)
reconcile   conciliar, cuadrar
reconciliation   ajuste (*m.*)
record   disco (*m.*); registrar
   — player   tocadiscos (*m.*)
red   rojo(a)
   — snapper   guachinango (*m.*) (*Méx.*)
   — wine   vino tinto (*f.*)
redheaded   pelirrojo(a)
reduce   rebajar
reduced   rebajado(a)
reduction   descuento (*m.*)
reference   referencia (*f.*)
referring to (a specific item)   por concepto (de)

refrigerator refrigerador (*m.*)

refund reembolso (*m.*)

refuse rehusar

regard: in — to en cuanto a, con referencia a

regarding por concepto (de)

register registro (*m.*); (*for school*) matricularse

registered brand marca registrada (*f.*)

registered letter carta certificada (*f.*), certificado (*m.*)

registration matrícula (*f.*)

   — card tarjeta de registro (*f.*); tarjeta de huésped (*f.*)

   — fees matrícula (*f.*)

regret lamentar, sentir (e:i)

regulation regulación (*f.*), disposición (*f.*)

reimbursement reembolso (*m.*)

related relacionado(a)

relation relación (*f.*)

relationship (family) parentesco (*m.*)

relatives familiares (*m. pl.*)

relocate trasladar

remain quedarse

remember acordar(se) (de) (o:ue), recordar (o:ue)

remodel remodelar

remove quitar(se)

rent alquilar, rentar; alquiler (*m.*)

rented alquilado(a)

renter inquilino(a) (*m., f.*)

reorganize reorganizar

repair reparar; reparación (*f.*)

   — shop taller de mecánica (*m.*), taller de reparación (*m.*)

report informe (*m.*); rendir (e:i) informe, reportar; (*a crime*) denunciar

represent representar

reproduction réplica (*f.*)

request pedir (e:l)

require exigir, requerir (e:ie)

requirement requisito (*m.*)

reservation reservación (*f.*), reserva (*f.*)

reserve reservar

resident card tarjeta de residente (*f.*)

residential residencial

resign (from) renunciar (a)

respective correspondiente

responsible responsable

rest descansar

   the — los (las) demás

restaurant restaurante (*m.*), restorán (*m.*)

restitution restitución (*f.*)

result resultar

resumé resumen (*m.*)

retail al detal, al detalle, por mayor; menudeo (*m.*)

retailer detallista (*m., f.*), minorista (*m.*)

retain (a lawyer) nombrar

retirement retiro (*m.*), jubilación (*f.*)

return regresar, volver (o:ue); (*give back*) devolver (o:ue)

   — receipt acuse de recibo (*m.*)

revenue renta (*f.*)

rice arroz (*m.*)

   — pudding arroz con leche (*m.*)

ride a bicycle montar en bicicleta

ride a horse montar a caballo

ridiculous ridículo(a)

right   derecho(a)
   —**?**   ¿verdad?
   — **away**   en seguida
   — **now**   ahora mismo
ring   anillo (*m.*), sortija (*f.*)
riot   motín (*m.*)
ripe   maduro(a)
risk   riesgo (*m.*)
river   río (*m.*)
roasted   asado(a)
rob   robar
robber   ladrón(ona) (*m., f.*)
robbery   robo (*m.*)
robe   bata (*f.*)
roll of film   rollo de película (*m.*)
roller bearings   cojinetes (*m. pl.*)
roof   techo (*m.*)
   — **tile**   teja (*f.*)
room   cuarto (*m.*), habitación (*f.*), sala (*f.*),
   recámara (*f.*) (*Méx.*)
   — **service**   servicio de habitación (*m.*)
round (boxing)   asalto (*m.*)
round trip   de ida y vuelta
   — **ticket**   pasaje (billete) de ida y vuelta (*m.*)
route   ruta (*f.*)
row   fila (*f.*)
rubber band   banda elástica (*f.*), goma (*f.*)
   (*Puerto Rico*), liga (*f.*) (*Méx. y Cuba*)
rudimentary   rudimentario(a)
rule out   descartar
rum   ron (*m.*)
run over   atropellar

S

sacrifice (oneself)   sacrificar(se)
safe   seguro(a)
saint's day   día del santo (*m.*)
salad   ensalada (*f.*)
salary   sueldo (*m.*), salario (*m.*)
sale   liquidación (*f.*), venta (*f.*)
sales   ventas (*f. pl.*)
  — **manager**   jefe(a) de ventas (*m., f.*)
  — **tax**   impuesto sobre la venta (*m.*)
salmon   salmón (*m.*)
salon   peluquería (*f.*), salón de belleza (*m.*)
salt   sal (*f.*)
salutation   saludo (*m.*)
same   mismo(a)
  — **as**   igual (que)
sample   muestra (*f.*); ejemplar (*m.*)
sandal   sandalia (*f.*)
sandwich   sándwich (*m.*)
satisfied   satisfecho(a)
Saturday   sábado (*m.*)
sauce   salsa (*f.*)
saucer   platillo (*m.*)
sausage   salchicha (*f.*)
save   ahorrar
saving   ahorro (*m.*)
savings   ahorros (*m. pl.*)
  — **account**   cuenta de ahorros (*f.*)
say   decir (e:i)
  — **no**   decir que no
  — **yes**   decir que sí
scales   balanza (*f.*)
scanner   escáner (*m.*), escanógrafo (*m.*)

scarcely   apenas
schedule   horario (*m.*), itinerario (*m.*)
scholarship   beca (*f.*)
school   escuela (*f.*)
schooling   carrera (*f.*)
scrambled   revuelto(a)
scream   gritar
screen   pantalla (*f.*)
scrub   fregar (e:ie)
sea bass   corbina (*f.*)
seafood   mariscos (*m. pl.*)
seasick   mareado(a)
seasickness   mareo (*m.*)
season   estación (*f.*)
seat   asiento (*m.*); sentar (e:ie)
second   segundo(a)
secretary   secretario(a) (*m., f.*)
section   sección (*f.*)
see   ver
  — after   encargarse (de)
  — you tomorrow.   Hasta mañana.
seem   parecer
select   elegir (e:i), escoger, seleccionar
sell   vender
  — well   venderse bien
selling price   precio de venta (*m.*)
semester   semestre (*m.*)
send   enviar, mandar
sender   remitente (*m., f.*)
separate   separado(a)
separately   aparte
September   septiembre
serious   grave, serio(a)
servant   sirviente(a) (*m., f.*)

serve servir (e:i)
service servicio (*m.*)
   — station estación de servicio (*f.*), gasolinera (*f.*)
set (in place) disponer
   — fire to prender fuego a
   — the table poner la mesa
   — up a business poner (abrir) un negocio
seven siete
several (with nouns) unos(as), varios(as)
shampoo champú (*m.*), lavado (*m.*)
share acción (*f.*)
shave afeitar(se)
shaver máquina de afeitar (*f.*)
she ella (*f.*)
sheet sábana (*f.*)
shelf estante (*m.*)
shellfish marisco (*m.*)
shift turno (*m.*)
ship barco (*m.*), buque (*m.*)
shipment carga (*f.*), cargamento (*m.*)
shipping transporte (*m.*)
shock absorber amortiguador (*m.*)
shoe zapato (*m.*)
   — store zapatería (*f.*)
shop establecimiento (*m.*)
   — window escaparate (*m.*), vidriera (*f.*)
shopping center centro comercial (*m.*)
short (height) bajo(a)
shot inyección (*f.*)
should deber
shoulder hombro (*m.*)
shout gritar

show   enseñar, mostrar (o:ue); demostración (f.)
  — a film   pasar una película
shower   ducha (f.), regadera (f.) (Méx.); ducharse
showroom   salón de exhibición (m.)
shrimp   camarón (m.), gamba (f.) (España)
sick   enfermo(a)
sickness   enfermedad (f.)
side   lado (m.)
sidewalk   acerca (f.), banqueta (f.) (Méx.),
  vereda (f.)
sign   firmar; señal (f.)
signal   señal (f.)
signature   firma (f.)
silver   plata (f.)
since   pues; desde que
single   soltero(a)
sir   señor (m.)
sit down   sentar(se) (e:ie)
situated   situado(a)
six   seis
  — hundred   seiscientos(as)
size   medida (f.), talla (f.), tamaño (m.)
skate   patinar
ski   esquiar
skirt   falda (f.)
skycap   maletero(a) (m., f.)
sleep   dormir (o:ue)
sleeping bag   bolsa de dormir (f.)
slim   delgado(a)
slogan   lema (m.)
slow   despacio
small   chico(a), pequeño(a)
  — Business Administration
    Administración de Pequeños Negocios (f.)

— **change** calderilla (*f.*), moneda
   fraccionaria (*f.*), menudo (*m.*) (*Cuba*), suelto
   (*m.*) (*Puerto Rico*)

smoke fumar; humo (*m.*)

smoker fumador(a) (*m.*, *f.*)

smoking (no smoking) section sección de
   fumar (no fumar) (*f.*)

snow storm nevada (*f.*)

so así que, tan

— **many** tantos(as)

— **much** tanto(a)

— **not much** no tanto(a)

— **that** de modo que, para que

soap jabón (*m.*)

soccer fútbol (*m.*)

social social

— **Security** Seguro Social (*m.*)

socket enchufe (*m.*)

socks calcetines (*m. pl.*)

soda pop gaseosa (*f.*), refresco (*m.*)

sofa sofá (*m.*)

soft drink gaseosa (*f.*), refresco (*m.*)

soft-boiled pasado(a) por agua

software soporte lógico (*m.*)

sole lenguado (*m.*)

solve resolver (o:ue)

some algún(o)(a); (*with nouns*) unos(as)

somebody alguien

someone alguien

something algo

sometimes a veces, algunas veces

son hijo (*m.*)

soon pronto

sophisticated sofisticado(a)

sore throat   dolor de garganta (*m.*)
sorry: I'm —.   Lo siento.
soup   sopa (*f.*)
south   sur (*m.*)
southeast   sureste (*m.*)
southwest   suroeste (*m.*)
Spain   España
Spaniard   español(a) (*m., f.*)
spare part   pieza de repuesto (*f.*), repuesto (*m.*)
spark plug   bujía (*f.*)
speak   hablar
special   especial
   — delivery   entrega especial (*f.*)
specialist   especialista (*m., f.*)
specialization   especialización (*f.*)
specialty   especialidad (*f.*)
specification   indicación (*f.*)
speed   velocidad (*f.*)
   — limit   velocidad máxima (*f.*)
speeding   exceso de velocidad (*m.*)
spend   gastar
spinach   espinaca (*f.*)
spite: in — of (the fact that)   a pesar de (que)
sport   deporte (*m.*)
spread sheet   hoja de análisis (*f.*), hoja de cálculo (*f.*)
sprinkler system   sistema de regadío (*m.*)
square   cuadrado(a)
squeeze   apretar (e:ie)
squid   calamar (*m.*)
stable   estable
stained   manchado(a)
stair(s)   escalera (*f.*)

stamp (postage)   estampilla (*f.*), sello (*m.*), timbre (*m.*) (*Méx.*)

stand in line   hacer cola

standard: — shift   cambio mecánico (*m.*); (*adj.*) de cambios mecánicos

— **deduction**   deducción general (*f.*)

staple   grapa (*f.*), presilla (*f.*) (*Cuba*)

stapler   grapadora (*f.*), presilladora (*f.*) (*Cuba*)

start   empezar (e:ie); (*a motor*) arrancar

starting   a partir de

starve   morirse (o:ue) de hambre

state   estado (*m.*)

— **tax**   impuesto estatal (del estado) (*m.*)

statement of account   estado de cuenta (*m.*)

station   estación (*f.*)

statistics   estadística (*f.*)

stay   quedarse

— **home**   quedarse en casa

steak   bife (*m.*), biftec (*m.*), bisté (*m.*), bistec (*m.*); carne asada (*f.*)

steal   robar

steamed   al vapor

steering wheel   timón (*m.*), volante (*m.*)

step   paso (*m.*)

a — **further**   un paso más

stew   guisado (*m.*), guiso (*m.*)

stewardess   azafata (*f.*)

stewed   estofado(a), guisado(a)

stick out one's tongue   sacar la lengua

still   todavía

stock   acción (*f.*)

stocking   media (*f.*)

stomach   estómago (*m.*)

stone   piedra (*f.*)

stop alto (*m.*); parar; (*a motor*) apagar; (*doing something*) dejar de (+ *inf.*)
  — over escala (*f.*)
  — sign señal de parada (*f.*)
store tienda (*f.*), bazar (*m.*)
  — window vidriera (*f.*), escaparate (*m.*)
story piso (*m.*)
stove cocina (*f.*)
stranger desconocido(a) (*m., f.*)
strawberries fresas (*f. pl.*)
street calle (*f.*)
strong fuerte
structure estructura (*f.*)
stucco estuco (*m.*)
student estudiante (*m., f.*)
studies carrera (*f.*)
study estudiar
stuffed relleno(a)
subject asunto (*m.*); (*in school*) asignatura (*f.*), materia (*f.*)
subtotal subtotal (*m.*)
subway subterráneo (*m.*)
success éxito (*m.*)
such a tan
suckling pig lechón (*m.*)
sue poner una demanda, demandar
suffer sufrir
suffering sufrimiento (*m.*)
sufficient suficiente
sugar azúcar (*m.*)
suggest sugerir (e:ie)
suggestive sugestivo(a); sugerente
suicide suicidio (*m.*)
suit traje (*m.*); convenir

it suits (me, him, etc.) (me, le, etc.) conviene

suitcase maleta (*f.*), valija (*f.*)

summer verano (*m.*)

sunglasses anteojos de sol (*m. pl.*), gafas de sol (*f. pl.*)

sunken hundido(a)

sunny soleado(a)

suntan lotion bronceador (*m.*)

supermarket supermercado (*m.*); hipermercado (*m.*)

superstitious supersticioso(a)

supper cena (*f.*)

supplier proveedor(a) (*m., f.*), suministrador(a) (*m., f.*)

suppose suponer

sure (*adv.*) bueno; (*adj.*) seguro(a)

surname apellido (*m.*)

surpass sobrepasar

surrender value rescate (*m.*)

survey sondeo de opinión pública (*m.*), encuesta (*f.*)

suspect sospechar

suspension sistema de suspensión (*m.*)

sweater suéter (*m.*)

sweep barrer

sweets dulces (*m. pl.*)

swim nadar

swimming natación (*f.*)

swimming pool piscina (*f.*); alberca (*f.*) (*Méx.*)

symptom síntoma (*m.*)

syrup jarabe (*m.*)

system sistema (*m.*); medios (*m. pl.*)

T

table   mesa (*f.*)
tablecloth   mantel (*m.*)
tailor   sastre (*m.*)
take   coger; llevar; quedarse (con); tomar; (*a bus, train, etc.*) tomar
   — **a deep breath**   respirar hondo
   — **advantage (of)**   aprovechar
   — **an X-ray**   hacer una radiografía
   — **away**   quitar; llevarse
   — **charge (of)**   encargarse (de)
   — **insurance**   sacar seguro
   — **off**   quitar(se); (*a plane*) despegar
   — **out**   sacar
   — **place**   tener lugar; efectuarse
   — **responsibility for**   responsabilizarse
   — **someone or something someplace**
     llevar
   — **the trash out**   sacar la basura
   — **time**   demorar
talk   hablar, conversar, charlar, platicar
tall   alto(a)
tank   tanque (*m.*)
tape recorder   grabadora (*f.*)
tare   tara (*f.*)
tariff   tarifa (*f.*)
taste   al gusto
tasty   rico(a), sabroso(a)
tattoo   tatuaje (*m.*)
tax   impuesto (*m.*)
   — **evasion**   evasión fiscal (*f.*)
   — **payer**   contribuyente (*m., f.*)
   — **rate table**   escala de impuestos (*f.*)

— **return**   declaración de impuestos (*f.*), planilla de contribución sobre ingresos (*f.*) (*Puerto Rico*)

taxable income   ingresos sujetos a impuestos (*m. pl.*)

taxi   taxi (*m.*)

— **driver**   taxista (*m., f.*)

— **stop**   parada de taxi (*f.*)

taximeter   taxímetro (*m.*)

tea   té (*m.*)

teach   enseñar

team   equipo (*m.*)

technician   técnico(a) (*m., f.*)

telecommunications   telecomunicaciones (*f. pl.*)

telegram   telegrama (*m.*)

telegraphy   telegrafía (*f.*)

telephone   teléfono (*m.*)

— **operator**   telefonista (*m., f.*), operador(a) (*m., f.*)

television   televisión (*f.*)

— **set**   televisor (*m.*)

tell   decir (e:i)

temperature   temperatura (*f.*)

ten   diez

tennis   tenis (*m.*)

tent   tienda de campaña (*f.*)

term   plazo (*m.*); término (*m.*)

— **of payment**   condición de pago (*f.*)

termite   comején (*m.*), termita (*f.*)

terrace   terraza (*f.*)

test   análisis (*m.*), examen (*m.*), prueba (*f.*)

tetanus   tétano (*m.*)

— **shot**   inyección antitetánica (*f.*)

than   que

thank you (very much) (muchas) gracias
that aquel(la); ese(a); eso; lo que; que; ése (*m.*);
   aquélla, ésa (*f.*)
  — includes . . . Eso incluye…
  — is to say es decir
  — one (over there) aquél
  — which lo (la) que
  —'s all. Eso es todo.
  —'s good! ¡Qué bueno!
  —'s why por eso
theater teatro (*m.*)
theft robo (*m.*)
their su(s); suyo(a)(os)(as)
then entonces, luego
there allá, allí
  — are all kinds of things hay de todo
  — is (are) hay
  —'s no hurry. No hay apuro (prisa).
therefore por eso
these estos(as)
they ellos(as) (*m., f.*)
thief ladrón(ona) (*m., f.*)
thin delgado(a)
thing cosa (*f.*)
think creer, pensar (e:ie)
  — about pensar (e:ie) en
third tercer(o)(a)
  — party tercera persona (*f.*); tercero(a) (*m., f.*)
thirst sed (*f.*)
thirteen trece
thirty treinta
this este(a)
  — time esta vez
  — very day hoy mismo

— **way** por aquí
those los(las) de
thousand mil
threaten amenazar
three tres
— **hundred** trescientos(as)
throat garganta (*f.*)
through por; mediante
throw away botar
thumbtack chinche (*f.*), tachuela (*f.*) (*Puerto Rico*)
Thursday jueves (*m.*)
ticket billete (*m.*), boleto (*m.*), pasaje (*m.*); (*fine*) multa (*f.*)
— **office** despacho de boletos (*m.*)
tie (the score) empatar
tied up inmovilizado(a)
tile losa (*f.*), baldosa (*f.*)
time época (*f.*); hora (*f.*); tiempo (*m.*); vez (*f.*)
— **certificate** a plazo fijo
— **of arrival** hora de entrada (*f.*)
— **table** horario (*m.*), itinerario (*m.*)
tip propina (*f.*)
tire llanta (*f.*), goma (*f.*), neumático (*m.*)
title título (*m.*), carga (*f.*)
to a, para
— **order** al gusto
— **taste** al gusto
— **the left** a la izquierda
— **the right** a la derecha
— **us** nos
toast (*with champagne*) brindis (*m.*); pan tostado (*m.*), tostada (*f.*)
toaster tostadora (*f.*)

today hoy
toe dedo (del pie) (*m.*)
together juntos(as)
— **with** junto con
toilet inodoro (*m.*)
— **paper** papel higiénico (*m.*)
token ficha (*f.*)
toll tarifa (*f.*)
tomato tomate (*m.*)
— **juice** jugo de tomate (*m.*)
— **sauce** salsa de tomate (*f.*)
tomorrow mañana
ton tonelada (*f.*)
tongue lengua (*f.*)
tonight esta noche
too demasiado(a); también
— **bad!** ¡Paciencia!
— **much** demasiado(a)
tooth diente (*m.*)
— **paste** pasta dentífrica (*f.*)
top quality de primera calidad, de primera
torn roto(a)
tornado tornado (*m.*)
tortilla tortilla (*f.*) (*Méx.*)
total total (*m.*)
totally totalmente
tour excursión (*f.*)
tourist turista (*m., f.*)
— **guide** guía para turistas (*f.*)
— **office** oficina de turismo (*f.*)
tow remolcar
— **truck** grúa (*f.*), remolcador (*m.*)
toward hacia
— **here** para acá

towel toalla (*f.*)

town pueblo (*m.*)

— **square** plaza (*f.*)

toy shop juguetería (*f.*)

trademark marca registrada (*f.*)

traffic tráfico (*m.*), tránsito (*m.*)

— **law** ley de tránsito (tráfico) (*f.*)

— **light** semáforo (*m.*)

— **officer** policía de tránsito (tráfico) (*m., f.*)

— **sign** señal de tráfico (*f.*)

train ferrocarril (*m.*), tren (*m.*)

transaction transacción (*f.*)

transfer transferencia (*f.*), tra(n)sbordo (*m.*),
traspaso (*m.*); tra(n)sbordar

transformer transformador (*m.*)

transit tránsito (*m.*)

translator traductor(a) (*m., f.*)

transmission transmisión (*f.*)

— **fluid** líquido de transmisión (*m.*)

transparent transparente

transport transporte (*m.*); transportar

trash basura (*f.*)

— **can** lata de la basura (*f.*)

travel viajar; viaje (*m.*)

— **agency** agencia de viajes (*f.*)

traveler's check cheque de viajero (*m.*)

traveling salesperson viajante (*m., f.*), agente
viajero(a) (*m., f.*)

tray bandeja (*f.*)

tree árbol (*m.*)

trespassing entrada ilegal (*f.*)

trial juicio (*m.*)

— **balance** balance de comprobación (*m.*)

trip viaje (*m.*)

trousers pantalones (*m. pl.*)

trout trucha (*f.*)

truck camión (*m.*)

true verdadero(a)

  —? ¿Verdad?

trunk baúl (*m.*); (*of a car*) cajuela (*f.*) (*Méx.*), maletero (*m.*)

truth verdad (*f.*)

try probar (o:ue)

  — **on** probar(se) (o:ue)

  — **to** tratar de

Tuesday martes (*m.*)

tuition matrícula (*f.*)

tuna atún (*m.*), bonito (*m.*)

turbulence turbulencia (*f.*)

turkey pavo (*m.*), guajolote (*m.*) (*Méx.*), guanajo (*m.*) (*Cuba*)

turn doblar; voltear

  — **off** apagar

  — **on** encender (e:ie)

  — **up the volume** subir el volumen

TV set televisor (*m.*)

twelve doce

twenty veinte

twice doble (*m.*)

twist torcer (o:ue)

two dos

type tipo (*m.*)

typewriter máquina de escribir (*f.*)

typical típico(a)

typist mecanógrafo(a) (*m., f.*)

U

ugly   feo(a)
uncomfortable   incómodo(a)
under   debajo de
underdeveloped   subdesarrollado(a)
underneath   debajo (de)
understand   comprender, entender (e:ie)
underwear   ropa interior (*f.*)
unemployment   desempleo (*m.*)
unfortunately   desgraciadamente
unit   unidad (*f.*)
United States   Estados Unidos (*m. pl.*)
university   universidad (*f.*); (*adj.*)
   universitario(a)
unleaded gasoline   gasolina sin plomo (*f.*)
unless   a menos que
unload   descargar
unloading   descarga (*f.*)
unnecessary   innecesario(a)
until   hasta (que)
   — one hits (arrives at)   hasta llegar a
up to   hasta
upholstery   tapicería (*f.*), vestidura (*f.*)
upon arrival   a la llegada, al llegar
upper berth   litera alta (*f.*)
upstairs   arriba; planta alta (*f.*)
urgency   urgencia (*f.*)
use   usar, utilizar; uso (*m.*)
used   usado(a); de uso
uselessly   inútilmente
usual   de costumbre
   — terms in the market   las (condiciones) de
      costumbre en la plaza (*f. pl.*)

utilize utilizar

V

vacant desocupado(a), libre, vacío(a)
vacate desocupar
   — **a room** desocupar la habitación
vacation vacaciones (*f. pl.*)
vacuum pasar la aspiradora
   — **cleaner** aspiradora (*f.*)
valid válido(a)
valuable valioso(a)
value valor (*m.*); tasar
value-added tax (VAT) impuesto al valor
   agregado (*m.*) (I.V.A.)
van camioneta (*f.*)
vanilla vainilla (*f.*)
variable variable
variety variedad (*f.*)
various varios(as)
vary variar
VCR grabadora de vídeo (*f.*), casetera (*f.*),
   videograbadora (*f.*)
veal ternera (*f.*)
vegetable verdura (*f.*), vegetal (*m.*)
verb verbo (*m.*)
verification comprobante (*m.*)
version versión (*f.*)
very muy
   — **well** muy bien
vibration vibración (*f.*)
video camera cámara de vídeo (*f.*)
view vista (*f.*)
village square plaza (*f.*)

violation violación (f.)
visa visa (f.)
visit visitar
vitamin vitamina (f.)
vocabulary vocabulario (m.)
voice voz (f.)
volume volumen (m.)
vomit vomitar
voucher vale (m.)

W

wage and tax statement (W-2) comprobante del sueldo y de los descuentos (m.)
wait esperar
   — **for** esperar
   — **on** atender (e:ie)
waiter mesero (m.), mozo (m.), camarero (m.)
waitress mesera (f.), moza (f.), camarera (f.)
wake up despertar(se) (e:ie)
walk caminar
wallet billetera (f.)
want desear, querer (e:ie)
warehouse almacén (m.)
wash fregar (e:ie), lavar; (*oneself*) lavar(se)
washer lavadora (f.)
washing machine lavadora (f.)
watch reloj (m.)
water agua (f. but el agua)
   — **pump** bomba de agua (f.)
watercress berro (m.)
watermelon melón de agua (m.), sandía (f.)
weak débil
wear llevar puesto(a), usar

weave (car)   ir zigzagueando
Web page   página de la Web (*f.*)
wedding   boda (*f.*)
week   semana (*f.*)
weekday   día de semana (*m.*)
weekend   fin de semana (*m.*)
weekly   (*adj.*) semanal
weigh (oneself)   pesar(se)
weight   pesa (*f.*); peso (*m.*)
welcome   bienvenido(a)
  You're —.   De nada.
well   bien; bueno; pues
  — **done (meat)**   bien cocido(a), bien
    cocinado(a)
  — **established**   acreditado(a)
west   oeste (*m.*)
wet   mojado(a)
what   qué, cuál; lo que
  — **a coincidence!**   ¡Qué casualidad!
  — **a mess!**   ¡Qué lío!
  — **a pity!**   ¡Qué lástima!
  — **are (they) like?**   ¿Cómo son?
  — **can I do for you?**   ¿Qué se le ofrece?
  — **for?**   ¿Para qué?
  — **size shoe do you wear?**   ¿Qué número
    calza?
  — **time is it?**   ¿Qué hora es?
  — **will become of . . . ?**   ¿Qué será de... ?
  —**'s new?**   ¿Qué hay de nuevo?
  —**'s the rate of exchange?**   ¿A cómo está el
    cambio de moneda?
when   cuando
when?   ¿cuándo?
where   donde

where? ¿dónde?; ¿adónde?

whether si

which que

which? ¿qué?; ¿cuál?

while mientras

white blanco(a)

  — **wine** vino blanco (*m.*)

who? ¿quién?

wholesale al mayoreo, al por mayor

wholesaler mayorista (*m., f.*)

why? ¿por qué?

widow viuda (*f.*)

widower viudo (*m.*)

width ancho (*m.*)

wife esposa (*f.*)

will testamento (*m.*)

win ganar

window ventanilla (*f.*)

  — **seat** asiento de ventanilla (*m.*)

windshield parabrisas (*m. sing.*)

  — **wiper** limpiaparabrisas (*m. sing.*)

wine vino (*m.*)

winner ganador(a) (*m., f.*)

winter invierno (*m.*)

wish desear, querer (e:ie)

with con

  — **me** conmigo

  — **whom?** ¿con quién?

  — **whom would you like to speak?** ¿Con quién quieres hablar?

withdraw money sacar el dinero

withdrawal retiro (*m.*)

within dentro de

without   sin
  — **hope**   sin remedio
witness   testigo (*m., f.*)
woman   mujer (*f.*)
wonder   preguntarse
wood   madera (*f.*)
wool   lana (*f.*)
word processing   composición de textos (*f.*),
  procesamiento de textos (*m.*)
work   funcionar; trabajar; trabajo (*m.*)
workday   día de trabajo (*m.*), día hábil (*m.*), día
  laborable (*m.*)
worker   trabajador(a) (*m., f.*)
  —'**s compensation insurance**   seguro de
  accidentes de trabajo (*m.*)
world   mundo (*m.*)
  corporate —   el mundo de las empresas (*m.*)
  the — **over**   a todo el mundo
worldwide   mundial
worried   preocupado(a)
worry   preocuparse
worth   valor (*m.*)
wound   herida (*f.*)
wrap   envolver (o:ue)
wrapped   envuelto(a)
wrist   muñeca (*f.*)
wristwatch   reloj de pulsera (*m.*)
write   escribir
  — **a check**   extender (e:ie) un cheque, girar un
  cheque
  — **down**   anotar
writing paper   papel de carta (*m.*)

X

X-ray   radiografía (*f.*)

Y

year   año (*m.*)
yearly   (*adv.*) al año; (*adj.*) anual
yellow   amarillo(a)
yes   sí
yesterday   ayer
yet   todavía
yield   rendimiento (*m.*)
yogurt   yogur (*m.*)
you   (*fam.*) tú; (*form.*) Ud., usted; (*pl.*) Uds.,
   ustedes
   —'re welcome.   De nada.
young   joven
   — lady   señorita (*f.*)
   — man   chico (*m.*), joven (*m.*), muchacho (*m.*)
   — woman   chica (*f.*), joven (*f.*), muchacha (*f.*)
younger   menor
your   (*form.*) su(s); (*fam.*) tu(s)

Z

zone   zona (*f.*)